VEGAN KETO

THE AMAZING VEGAN KETO MAGIC

Simple Yet Delicious Plant Based Keto Meal Prep Recipes for Vegans and Vegetarians

JAMIE CHANEY

Table of Contents

PART I

Vegan Keto

The ketogenic diet is a popular diet that is low in carbohydrates and is high in fat. The diet involves moderate consumption of protein that can promote weight loss and can also help in the improvement of overall health. Although the keto diet is mostly associated with animal-based foods, it can also be adapted for fitting food items that are plant-based, specifically vegan diets. The vegan diet does not include any kind of animal product. But, with proper planning, even vegans can enjoy the benefits of the keto diet.

In keto diet, carbs are reduced to 45-50 grams per day for maintaining and reaching ketosis. Ketosis is a metabolic process of the body for burning fat as fuel in place of glucose. People who follow a vegan keto diet rely on plant-based foods such as grains, veggies, and fruits. As the requirement of fat is more, plant-based food products such as avocados, coconut oil, nuts, and seeds are included in the vegan keto diet. Vegan keto diet comes along with various benefits. It can reduce the overall risk of developing severe health conditions like diabetes, heart diseases, and specific cancers. For instance, studies revealed that all those who follow vegan keto diet have a 74% lower risk of high blood pressure and a 75% risk reduction for type 2 diabetes.

It has also been found that people who follow a vegan keto diet can lose more weight than those who eat animal-based food products. The vegan keto diet can also increase the level of adiponectin, a protein responsible for regulating blood sugar and fat metabolism. When the level of adiponectin is high, it can help in the reduction of inflammation, better control over blood sugar, and can also help in reducing diseases related to obesity. Keto diet has also shown evident results in reducing the risk factors of heart diseases, along with LDL cholesterol, blood pressure, and high triglycerides. Combining a vegan diet along with a ketogenic diet can effectively impact your overall health.

When you start following a vegan diet, you will need to reduce the intake of carbs and replace them with healthy fats. You will also need to include vegan high protein sources. You cannot consume animal-based products such as poultry, egg, meat, seafood, and dairy. Here are some examples of the food items that you will need to avoid altogether:

- **Dairy:** Butter, milk, yogurt

- **Poultry and meat:** Turkey, pork, beef, chicken

- **Egg:** Egg yolk and egg white

- **Animal-based items:** Whey protein, egg white protein, honey

- **Seafood:** Shrimp, fish, mussels, clams

Here are some examples of the food items that you will need to reduce:

- **Sugar-based drinks:** Soda, juice, sweet tea, sports drinks, smoothies

- **Starches and grains:** Bread, cereal, pasta, baked items

- **Starchy veggies:** Sweet potatoes, potatoes, beet, squash, peas

Turn to the next page for recipes that can help you get started with a vegan keto diet.

Chapter 1: Breakfast Recipes

Breakfast is an important part of any diet plan. Here are some tasty vegan keto recipes for you.

Tofu Scramble

Total Prep & Cooking Time: Twenty minutes

Yields: Two servings

Nutrition Facts: Calories: 204 | Protein: 21.3g | Carbs: 3.6g | Fat: 12.3g | Fiber: 0.8g

Ingredients:

- Two-hundred grams of tofu (firm)
- One tbsp. of vegan butter
- Two tbsps. of nutritional yeast
- Half tsp. of each
    - Paprika
    - Turmeric
    - Garlic powder
- One tsp. of Dijon mustard
- One-fourth tsp. of each
    - Onion powder
    - Black salt
- One-third cup of soy milk

Method:

1. Place tofu in a bowl. Use a fork for mashing the tofu. Leave some medium-sized chunks.

2. Add turmeric, yeast, paprika, garlic powder, Dijon mustard, onion powder, and black salt in a bowl. Combine the ingredients. Add soy milk and whisk properly for making a smooth sauce.

3. Add vegan butter to a medium pan. Add mashed tofu and fry it for two minutes until browned. Add prepared sauce to the mashed tofu. Combine well. Cook for five minutes until the sauce gets absorbed by the tofu.

4. Serve hot.

Low Carb Pancakes

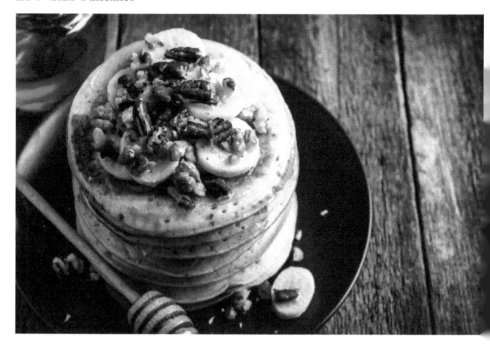

Total Prep & Cooking Time: Thirty minutes

Yields: Two servings

Nutrition Facts: Calories: 249 | Protein: 10.4g | Carbs: 12.8g | Fat: 19.6g | Fiber: 9.8g

Ingredients:

- Two tbsps. of almond butter
- One-fourth cup of almond milk (unsweetened)

- One tbsp. of coconut flour
- One and a half tbsps. of ground flax
- Half tsp. of baking powder

Method:

1. Take a small bowl and combine the almond milk with almond butter.

2. Take another bowl and combine the dry ingredients.

3. Add the mixture of milk to the dry mixture. Combine well. Allow the batter to sit for five minutes.

4. Heat a skillet over medium flame.

5. Add one spoon of batter to the warm skillet. Evenly spread out the batter—Cook the pancakes for five minutes on each side. Repeat the same for the remaining batter.

6. Serve the pancakes hot with almond butter from the top.

Cauliflower Hashbrowns

Total Prep & Cooking Time: Fifty minutes

Yields: Six servings

Nutrition Facts: Calories: 142 | Protein: 6.3g | Carbs: 18.2g | Fat: 5.6g | Fiber: 4.3g

Ingredients:

- Half head of cauliflower (separate the florets)
- One tbsp. of coconut oil
- Half onion (chopped)
- One-fourth cup of chickpea flour
- One tbsp. of cornstarch
- Half tsp. of each
  - Salt
  - Garlic powder
- Two tbsps. of water

Method:

1. Preheat your oven at 200 degrees Celsius; use parchment paper for lining a baking sheet. Spray the parchment paper with some oil.

2. Add onion and cauliflower in a blender and blend until crumbly.

3. Combine chickpea flour, cornstarch, salt, garlic powder, and water in a bowl. Mix well.

4. Add the cauliflower crumbles to the batter. Combine properly.

5. Shape the hashbrowns into thick patties.

6. Bake the hashbrowns in the oven for forty minutes. Flip the patties halfway.

7. Serve hot.

Vanilla Waffles

Total Prep & Cooking Time: Twenty minutes

Yields: Two servings

Nutrition Facts: Calories: 160 | Protein: 21.3g | Carbs: 13.6g | Fat: 4.9g | Fiber: 9.9g

Ingredients:

- One-fourth cup of oat flour
- Half scoop of protein powder (vanilla)
- One tbsp. of each
  - Flaxseed (ground)
  - Granulated sweetener of your choice
- One-fourth tsp. of baking powder
- Half cup of almond milk
- One-fourth tsp. of vanilla extract

Method:

1. Add the dry ingredients in a large bowl. Combine well.

2. Add baking powder, flaxseed, vanilla extract, and one-fourth cup of the almond milk in a bowl. Whisk well and allow it to sit for four minutes.

3. Add the dry ingredients to the mixture of vanilla extract. Combine properly.

4. Heat up a waffle iron and add two spoons of waffle mixture.

5. Cook for four minutes.

6. Serve hot.

Pecan And Cinnamon Porridge

Total Prep & Cooking Time: Twenty minutes

Yields: Two servings

Nutrition Facts: Calories: 580 | Protein: 13.4g | Carbs: 5.1g | Fat: 49.7g | Fiber: 10.8g

Ingredients:

- One-fourth cup of coconut milk
- One cup of almond butter
- Three-fourth cup of almond milk
- One tbsp. of coconut oil
- Two tbsps. of chia seeds
- Three tbsps. of hemp seeds
- One-fourth cup of each
    - Pecans
    - Flaked coconut
- Half tsp. of cinnamon

Method:

1. Mix almond milk, coconut milk, coconut oil, and almond butter in a pan. Simmer the mixture over a medium flame.

2. Once the mixture gets hot, remove from heat.

3. Add hemp seeds, chia seeds, pecans, and coconut flakes. Combine the ingredients and add cinnamon. Allow the porridge to sit for ten minutes.

4. Serve cold or hot with coconut flakes from the top.

Chapter 2: Appetizers Recipes

Appetizers play an important role in a complete meal. There are various vegan keto appetizers that you can include in your diet plan. Let's have a look at them.

Arugula Salad

Total Prep & Cooking Time: Ten minutes

Yields: Two servings

Nutrition Facts: Calories: 41 | Protein: 0.7g | Carbs: 2.6g | Fat: 3.1g | Fiber: 0.9g

Ingredients:

- Six tbsps. of olive oil (extra virgin)
- Two tbsps. of lemon juice
- Salt and pepper (according to taste)
- Four cups of arugula

Method:

1. Take a small-sized bowl and whisk together olive oil and lemon juice. Add pepper and salt.

2. Add the arugula in a large bowl and add the dressing from the top. Toss to combine.

Cauliflower Soup

Total Prep & Cooking Time: Thirty minutes

Yields: Four servings

Nutrition Facts: Calories: 127 | Protein: 5.2g | Carbs: 15.6g | Fat: 5.6g | Fiber: 3.9g

Ingredients:

- One tbsp. of olive oil (extra virgin)
- One yellow onion (chopped)

- One garlic clove (minced)
- One cauliflower (florets separated)
- Six cups of vegetable stock
- Three sprigs of thyme
- One bay leaf
- Pepper and salt (to taste)
- One-fourth cup of vegan cream

Method:

1. Take a deep pot and heat oil in it. Add onions and cook it for six minutes until tender. Add minced garlic to the pot. Add the florets of cauliflower, thyme, vegetable stock, and bay leaf. Simmer the mixture for twenty minutes until the florets are tender.

2. Remove bay leaf along with thyme. Blend the mixture using a stick blender until smooth. Add vegan cream and simmer for five minutes.

3. Serve with olive oil from the top.

Cauliflower Zucchini Fritters

Total Prep & Cooking Time: Twenty minutes

Yields: Eight servings

Nutrition Facts: Calories: 53 | Protein: 4.2g | Carbs: 5.9g | Fat: 2.1g | Fiber: 3.6g

Ingredients:

- Half head of a cauliflower
- Two large zucchinis
- One-fourth cup of flour
- Half tsp. of salt
- One-fourth tsp. of black pepper (ground)

Method:

1. Add zucchini in a blender and grate.

2. Add the cauliflower to the food processor and blend into small chunks.

3. Put the veggies in a dishtowel and squeeze out as much water as possible.

4. Transfer the veggies to a bowl; add flour, pepper, and salt. Mix well.

5. Shape the mixture into small patties.

6. Heat oil in a pan. Add the patties to the pan—Cook for three minutes on all sides.

7. Serve hot with any dipping sauce of your choice.

Notes:

- You can add chickpeas for extra flavor.

- The leftover fritters can be stored in the fridge for two days.

Zucchini Noodles And Avocado Sauce

Total Prep & Cooking Time: Thirty minutes

Yields: Two servings

Nutrition Facts: Calories: 311 | Protein: 6.7g | Carbs: 17.8g | Fat: 24.5g | Fiber: 9.9g

Ingredients:

- One large zucchini
- Two cups of basil
- One-third cup of water
- Four tbsps. of pine nuts
- Two tbsps. of lemon juice
- One large avocado
- Twelve cherry tomatoes (sliced)

Method:

1. Start with the zucchini noodles. Use a peeler or a spiralizer for making the noodles. In case you do not have a peeler or spiralizer, use a sharp knife for cutting thin strips of zucchini.

2. Add all the ingredients in the food processor except for the cherry tomatoes.

3. Combine sauce, noodles, and cherry tomatoes in a bowl. Toss for combining.

4. Serve at room temperature, or you can also chill in the freezer for ten minutes.

Notes:

- You can add any fresh herbs and veggies that you want to. You can replace zucchini with other vegetables such as carrots, cabbage, beet, squash, etc.

- Pine nuts can be replaced with any nuts of your choice.

- You can store the leftover noodles in the fridge for two days.

Roasted Brussels Sprouts

Total Prep & Cooking Time: Thirty minutes

Yields: Four servings

Nutrition Facts: Calories: 130 | Protein: 3.8g | Carbs: 11.3g | Fat: 9.7g | Fiber: 4.6g

Ingredients:

- Four-hundred grams of Brussels sprouts (halved)
- Two tbsps. of olive oil
- Black pepper and salt (according to taste)

Method:

1. Preheat your oven to 220 degrees Celsius.

2. Take a large baking sheet. Spread the Brussels sprouts on the sheet. Drizzle olive oil from the top. Season with pepper and salt. Toss for combining.

3. Roast the sprouts in the oven for twenty-five minutes until all the are crispy outside and tender from inside.

4. Serve hot.

Chapter 3: Main Course Recipes

After you are done with the appetizers, now it is time to have a look at the main course recipes. I have included some tasty vegan keto main course recipes in this section that you can enjoy in your lunch and dinner as well.

Mushroom Tomato Spaghetti Squash

Total Prep & Cooking Time: Forty minutes

Yields: Four servings

Nutrition Facts: Calories: 240 | Protein: 6.3g | Carbs: 21.3g | Fat: 8.9g | Fiber:

8.6g

Ingredients:

- Six cups of spaghetti squash (cooked)
- Two cups of tomatoes (diced)
- Four garlic cloves (minced)
- Eight ounces of mushrooms (sliced)
- One-third cup of onions (chopped)
- One-fourth cup of pine nuts (toasted)
- A handful of basil
- Three tbsps. of olive oil
- Black pepper and salt (for seasoning)

Method:

1. Cook the spaghetti squash in the way you like. The easiest way to cook is by roasting in the oven. When the squash is cool enough, remove the seeds along with the stringy bits. Shred the squash with a fork. Keep aside.

2. Take a sauté pan and heat some oil in it. Add mushrooms and onions to the pan. Keep cooking for four minutes until onion turns translucent. Add minced garlic to the pan and cook for two minutes. Add tomatoes and keep stirring.

3. Add the cooked spaghetti squash to the mixture and toss it well for combining. Add pine nuts and basil—season with salt and black pepper.

4. Serve hot.

Vegan Shakshuka
Total Prep & Cooking Time: Twenty-five minutes

Yields: Two servings

Nutrition Facts: Calories: 274 | Protein: 21.3g | Carbs: 22.6g | Fat: 9.5g | Fiber: 9.7g

Ingredients:

- One tbsp. of olive oil
- Four garlic cloves
- One can of diced tomatoes
- Pepper and salt (according to taste)
- Two tsps. of dried herbs
- Half tsp. of chili flakes (dried)
- One medium-sized block of tofu
- Black salt (optional)

Method:

1. Take a large skillet and add olive in it. Heat the oil and add garlic to the skillet. Brown the garlic a bit.

2. Add diced tomatoes, pepper, salt, chili flakes, and dried herbs. Mix the ingredients properly and simmer for five minutes.

3. Cut the tofu block in rounds and add them to the skillet.

4. Lower the flame and simmer the shakshuka for fifteen minutes. Cook until the sauce thickens, and the tofu rounds are tender.

5. Sprinkle some black salt from the top.

6. Serve with crusty bread slices or toast by the side.

Zucchini Lasagna

Total Prep & Cooking Time: One hour and twenty minutes

Yields: Eight servings

Nutrition Facts: Calories: 392 | Protein: 6.3g | Carbs: 18.7g | Fat: 33.9g | Fiber: 7.6g

Ingredients:

For vegan ricotta:

- Three cups of macadamia nuts (raw)
- Two tbsps. of nutritional yeast
- Half cup of basil (chopped)
- Two tsps. of oregano (dried)

- One medium-sized lemon (juiced)
- One tbsp. of olive oil (extra virgin)
- One tsp. of each
  - Black pepper
  - Salt
- One-third cup of water

Other ingredients:

- One jar of marinara sauce
- Three medium-sized zucchini squash (sliced thinly)

Method:

1. Preheat your oven at 160/175 degrees Celsius.

2. Add the nuts to a blender and blend. Scrape down the sides. Blend for making a fine meal.

3. Add yeast, oregano, basil, olive oil, lemon juice, pepper, water, and salt to the blended nuts in the blender. Blend for making a smooth paste.

4. Adjust the taste by adding seasonings. If you want more cheesiness, add yeast.

5. Pour one cup of marinara sauce in a baking dish. Line the dish with zucchini slices.

6. Add one scoop of ricotta mixture over the zucchini layer and spread evenly. Repeat for the remaining layers.

7. Cover the baking dish using foil and bake the lasagna for forty-five minutes. Remove the foil. Bake again for fifteen minutes.

8. Allow the lasagna to cool down for ten minutes.

9. Serve warm with basil from the top.

Arugula Tomato And Avocado Salad

Total Prep & Cooking Time: Fifteen minutes

Yields: Four servings

Nutrition Facts: Calories: 259 | Protein: 4.2g | Carbs: 5.2g | Fat: 17g | Fiber: 0.9g

Ingredients:

- One cup of cherry tomatoes (halved)
- Half cup of yellow cherry tomatoes (halved)
- Five ounces of arugula (chopped)
- Two large avocados (cut in chunks)
- Half cup of red onion (diced)
- Six leaves of basil (sliced)

For vinaigrette:

- Two tbsps. of balsamic vinegar
- One tbsp. of each:
  - Maple syrup
  - Olive oil
  - Lemon juice
- One clove of garlic (minced)
- Half tsp. of Italian seasoning
- One-fourth tsp. of each:
  - Pepper
  - Sea salt

Method:

1. Combine tomatoes, arugula, basil, red onion, and chunks of avocado in a mixing bowl.

2. Whisk together olive oil, lemon juice, vinegar, maple syrup, garlic, pepper, salt, and Italian seasoning in a small bowl. Mix well.

3. Add the dressing to the salad mix. Toss well for combining.

4. Serve with basil from the top.

Mushroom Fried Rice

Total Prep & Cooking Time: Thirty minutes

Yields: Six servings

Nutrition Facts: Calories: 118 | Protein: 10.2g | Carbs: 14.9g | Fat: 2.8g | Fiber: 7.3g

Ingredients:

- Four tbsps. of water
- One onion (diced)
- Two-inch piece of ginger (grated)
- Three cloves of garlic (minced)
- Ten ounces mix of veggies (carrots, peas, and edamame)
- Two cups of mushrooms (shitake)
- Four cups of cauliflower rice
- Three tbsps. of tamari
- Half tsp. of sesame oil
- One-fourth cup of green onion (sliced)

Method:

1. Take a large pan and add water to it. Sauté the onions in water for four minutes until translucent and soft; add ginger and garlic to the pan. Stir and cook the mixture for three minutes.

2. Add a mixture of veggies to the pan along with the mushrooms. Stir well for combining. Add the cauliflower rice and mix well. Let the fried rice cook for fifteen minutes until the water dissolves.

3. Add half tsp. of sesame oil and three tsps. of tamari. Stir again.

4. Serve hot with green onions from the top.

Note: You can store the leftover fried rice in the fridge for one day.

Chapter 4: Snacks And Dessert Recipes

Everyone loves to have some snacks in between their meals and a good dessert after having a sumptuous meal. So, I have included some tasty and easy snacks and dessert recipes in this section that you can include in your vegan keto diet.

Almond Flour Crackers

Total Prep & Cooking Time: Twenty-five minutes

Yields: Six servings

Nutrition Facts: Calories: 149 | Protein: 4.2g | Carbs: 5.7g | Fat: 12.3g | Fiber: 3.2g

Ingredients:

- One cup of almond flour
- Two tbsps. of sunflower seeds
- One tbsp. of flax meal or psyllium husks
- Three-fourth tsp. of sea salt
- Three tbsps. of water
- One tbsp. of coconut oil

Method:

1. Preheat your oven at 160/175 degrees Celsius.

2. Add sunflower seeds, almond flour, sea salt, and flax meal in a food processor. Process the ingredients.

3. Add the coconut oil along with water to the mixture and pulse again. Blend until a dough forms.

4. Add the dough on parchment paper and flatten the dough using your hands. Cover the cracker dough using another parchment paper and flatten with the help of a rolling pin.

5. Remove the upper layer sheet of parchment paper. Cut the dough into several crackers into the size and shape that you want.

6. Sprinkle some sea salt from the top.

7. Bake the crackers for fifteen minutes at 175 degrees Celsius until the edges are crisp and brown.

Guacamole

Total Prep & Cooking Time: Twenty minutes

Yields: Four servings

Nutrition Facts: Calories: 180.2 | Protein: 2.3g | Carbs: 12.1g | Fat: 15.2g | Fiber: 7.9g

Ingredients:

- Three ripe avocados
- Half onion (diced)
- Two tomatoes (diced)
- Three tbsps. of cilantro (chopped)
- One jalapeno pepper (diced)
- Two cloves of garlic (minced)
- One lime (juiced)
- Half tsp. of sea salt

Method:

1. Slice the avocado and remove the pit. Skin them and place them in a bowl.

2. Use a fork for mashing the avocados. You can either make it smooth or chunky.

3. Add remaining ingredients and mix well.

4. Serve with crackers.

Strawberry And Avocado Ices

Total Prep & Cooking Time: One hour and ten minutes

Yields: Four servings

Nutrition Facts: Calories: 93 | Protein: 3.1g | Carbs: 4.2g | Fat: 7.2g | Fiber: 4g

Ingredients:

- Two-hundred grams of strawberries (chopped)
- One avocado (chopped)
- Two tsps. of balsamic vinegar
- Half tsp. of vanilla extract
- Two tsps. of maple syrup

Method:

1. Add avocado, strawberries, vanilla, and vinegar in a bowl. Use a hand blender for pulsing the mixture. You can also use a food processor. Blend for reaching the consistency that you want. Add maple syrup and mix again.

2. Pour the mixture into small containers and add strawberry slices from the top. Cover the containers using a plastic wrap.

3. Freeze the containers for one hour.

4. Allow the containers to sit at room temperature for five minutes before serving.

Chocolate And Peanut Butter Ice Cream

Total Prep & Cooking Time: Three hours and ten minutes

Yields: Six servings

Nutrition Facts: Calories: 360 | Protein: 5.8g | Carbs: 7.9g | Fat: 34g | Fiber: 4.2g

Ingredients:

- One can of coconut milk
- Half cup of each
    - Powdered sweetener of your choice
    - Peanut butter
- One-third cup of coconut oil
- One-fourth cup of cocoa powder
- One pinch of salt

Method:

1. Add the ingredients in a blender. Keep blending until smooth.

2. Pour the ice cream mixture in a glass container. Cover the container and freeze for half an hour.

3. Remove the cover and stir the mixture, especially from the sides right to the center. Cover again and freeze for thirty minutes. Stir the mixture once again and freeze for two hours.

4. Scoop the ice cream into serving bowls and garnish with peanut butter from the top.

Carrot Cake

Total Prep & Cooking Time: One hour

Yields: Six servings

Nutrition Facts: Calories: 150 | Protein: 3.1g | Carbs: 4.1g | Fat: 6.3g | Fiber: 3.2g

Ingredients:

- Two cups of flour
- One and a half cup of almond flour
- One-fourth tsp. of baking soda
- One tbsp. of cinnamon
- One tsp. of nutmeg
- One carrot (shredded)
- One-third cup of walnuts (chopped)
- Two tbsps. of shredded coconut
- Half tbsp. of apple cider vinegar
- Three-fourth cup of vegan milk (any vegan milk of your choice)
- Half cup of olive oil
- One-fourth cup of maple syrup

Method:

1. Start by preheating your oven at 180 degrees Celsius. Use parchment paper for lining a square baking pan.

2. Combine maple syrup, olive oil, milk of your choice, and vinegar in a bowl. Add walnuts, carrots, and coconut to the mixture. Mix well.

3. Add flour, almond flour, spices, and baking soda. Combine the ingredients.

4. Pour the prepared batter in the lined pan. Bake the mixture for half an hour.

5. Allow the cake to cool down for five minutes.

6. Serve warm with a frosting of your choice.

Notes:

- Before baking the cake, add some shredded carrots from the top for extra flavor. It will make the cake look beautiful, as well.

- In case you have any leftover cake, you can store it in the fridge for one day.

- You can use almond milk for the best results.

Almond And Chocolate Pudding

Total Prep & Cooking Time: Five hours and ten minutes Yields: Three servings

Nutrition Facts: Calories: 280 | Protein: 5.2g | Carbs: 11.7g | Fat: 21.6g | Fiber: 8.9g

Ingredients:

- Two cups of almond milk
- Half cup of coconut cream
- Three tbsps. of vegan sweetener (of your choice)
- One avocado (pitted)
- Three tbsps. of cocoa powder
- One tsp. of vanilla extract
- Two tsps. of almond extract
- Sliced almonds (to garnish)

Method:

1. Add the listed ingredients in a high-power food processor. Blend the ingredients until smooth.

2. Pour the mixture into serving cups. Cover the cups and refrigerate for about five hours.

3. Serve with sliced almonds from the top.

Notes:

- This pudding is gluten-free and is ketogenic as well.
- You can add chocolate chips from the top for extra flavor.
- You can store the leftover pudding in the fridge for two days.

PART II

Vegan Cookbook

The vegan diet has gained immense popularity in the past few years. With an increasing number of participants, people have made up their mind to opt for the vegan options for health, environmental, or ethical reasons. When done in the perfect way, a vegan diet can help in showcasing a wide array of health benefits, for example, better control over blood sugar and a slimmer waistline. However, when a diet is based entirely on plant derivatives, it can result in a nutrient deficiency in various cases.

Veganism is being defined as a simple way of living that aims at excluding all major forms of animal cruelty and exploitation, whether for daily food, clothing, or some other purpose. For all these reasons, this diet does not include any form of animal products, such as eggs, dairy, and meat. It has been found that all those people who tend to practice veganism are thinner and also comes with a lower BMI or body mass index when compared with non-vegans. This can easily explain the primary reason why the majority of the people are turning to this form of diet as the only way for losing extra weight.

Adopting a vegan diet can help keep the blood sugar level under proper check and type 2 diabetes. According to some studies, vegans tend to benefit from the lower levels of blood sugar, higher sensitivity to insulin, and about 77% lower risk of developing diabetes than the non-vegans. The majority of the advantages can be easily explained by the increased consumption of fiber, which can blunt the blood sugar response. Several observational studies reported that vegans could have a 74% lower risk of having increased blood pressure along with a 43% lower risk of suffering from any chronic heart disease.

There is a specific food group that you will need to omit for following a vegan diet. This group of foods includes:

- **Poultry and meat:** Lamb, beef, veal, pork, organ meat, chicken, wild meat, goose, turkey, duck, etc.

- **Dairy:** Yogurt, butter, milk, cheese, ice cream, cream, etc.

- **Seafood and fish:** Fish of all types, squid, anchovies, calamari, shrimp, lobster, mussels, crab, etc.

- **Eggs:** From ostrich, chicken, fish, quail, etc.

- **Products from bees:** Bee pollen, honey, royal jelly, etc.

- **Ingredients based on animals:** Casein, whey, egg white albumen, shellac, lactose, gelatin, L-cysteine, isinglass, omega-3 fatty acids derived from fish, vitamin D3 derived from animals, and carmine.

You can opt for alternatives such as legumes, seitan, tofu, seeds, nut butter, nuts, veggies, fruits, whole grains, etc. The cooking style will remain the same, and the only difference will be the ingredients you are going to use.

Chapter 1: Breakfast Recipes

Breakfast is an essential meal of the day that needs to be fulfilled properly. Here are some vegan breakfast recipes for you.

Shamrock Sandwich

Total Prep & Cooking Time: Fifteen minutes

Yields: One serving

Nutrition Facts: Calories: 562 | Protein: 23g | Carbs: 43.2g | Fat: 31g | Fiber: 8.3g

Ingredients:

- One sausage patty (vegan)
- One cup of kale
- Two tsps. of olive oil (extra virgin)
- One tbsp. of pepitas
- Pepper and salt (according to taste)

For the sauce:

- One tbsp. of vegan mayonnaise
- One tsp. of jalapeno (chopped)
- One-fourth tsp. of paprika (smoky)

Other ingredients:

- One-fourth of an avocado (sliced)
- One toasted English muffin

Method:

1. Start by toasting the English muffin and keep it aside.

2. Take a sauté pan and drizzle some oil in it. Add the sausage patty and cook for two minutes on each side.

3. Add pepitas and kale to the hot pan. Add pepper and salt for adjusting the taste. When the kale gets soft, and the patty gets browned, remove the pan from heat.

4. Combine the spicy sauce.

5. Assemble the sandwich with sauce on the muffins and add the patty, avocado, pepitas, and kale.

Breakfast Burrito
Total Prep & Cooking Time: Thirty minutes

Yields: Two servings

Nutrition Facts: Calories: 618 | Protein: 20.3g | Carbs: 113g | Fat: 13.7g | Fiber: 21g

Ingredients:

- Three-fourth cup of rice (rinsed)
- Two cups of water
- One-fourth tsp. of salt
- One tbsp. of lime juice
- Half cup of cilantro (chopped)

For onions and hash browns:

- Half red onion
- Four red potatoes
- Two tbsp. of olive oil
- One-fourth tsp. of each
  - o Black pepper (ground)
  - o Salt

For black beans:

- One cup of black beans (cooked)
- One-fourth tsp. of each
  - o Chili powder
  - o Cumin powder
  - o Garlic powder

For the avocado slaw:

- One avocado
- Two tbsps. of lime juice
- One cup of green cabbage (sliced thinly)
- One jalapeno (sliced)
- Half tsp. of each
  - Black pepper
  - Salt

For serving:

- Two flour tortillas
- Half avocado (ripe, sliced)
- One-fourth cup of salsa

Method:

1. Boil water, salt, and rice in a pan. Simmer the mixture for twenty minutes until the rice turns fluffy. Drain and keep aside.

2. Heat oil in a pan. Chop the potatoes into small pieces and slice the onions in rings. Add the potatoes along with the onions to the pan. Add pepper and salt for seasoning; toss the mixture for five minutes. Keep aside.

3. Prepare the beans in a saucepan over a medium flame.

4. For making the slaw, mix lime juice and avocado in a bowl. Mash the avocado and mix. Add jalapeno, cabbage, and toss for combining. Add pepper and salt for seasoning.

5. Add cilantro and lime juice to the rice and combine using a fork.

6. Warm the tortillas in a pan or microwave for twenty seconds.

7. Add the prepared fillings to the tortillas in order of your choice and top with salsa; add sliced avocado from the top. Roll the tortillas and slice in half.

8. Serve with extra black beans and potatoes by the side.

Gingerbread Waffles

Total Prep & Cooking Time: Fifteen minutes

Yields: Six servings

Nutrition Facts: Calories: 170 | Protein: 4.2g | Carbs: 27.3g | Fat: 4.7g | Fiber: 3.9g

Ingredients:

- One cup of flour
- One tbsp. of flax seeds (ground)

- Two tsps. of baking powder
- One-fourth tsp. of each
  - Salt
  - Baking soda
- One tsp. of cinnamon (ground)
- One and a half tsps. of ginger (ground)
- Four tbsps. of brown sugar
- One cup of any non-dairy milk
- Two tbsps. of apple cider vinegar
- Two tbsps. of molasses
- One and a half tbsps. of olive oil

Method:

1. Preheat a waffle iron and grease it.

2. Put the dry ingredients in a mixing bowl and combine well.

3. Combine the wet ingredients in a medium mixing bowl or jug. Mix well until properly combined.

4. Add the mixture of wet ingredients into the dry mixture and mix well. The batter needs to be thick. In case the batter is excessively thick, you can add two tbsps. of non-dairy milk to the batter and mix.

5. Pour the batter in batches in the waffle iron and cook until steam stops to come out from the sides.

6. Open the waffle iron and take out the waffle carefully.

7. Serve warm.

Green Chickpeas And Toast
Total Prep & Cooking Time: Thirty minutes

Yields: Two servings

Nutrition Facts: Calories: 189 | Protein: 11.3g | Carbs: 27.1g | Fat: 3.2g | Fiber: 9.3g

Ingredients:

- Two tbsps. of olive oil
- Three shallots (diced)
- One-fourth tsp. of paprika (smoked)
- Two cloves of garlic (diced)
- Half tsp. of each
  - Sweet paprika
  - Salt
  - Cinnamon
  - Sugar
- Black pepper (according to taste)
- Two tomatoes (skinned)
- Two cups of chickpeas (cooked)
- Four crusty bread slices

Method:

1. Take a medium pan and heat oil in it.

2. Add the diced shallots to the oil and stir-fry. Add garlic to the pan. Cook for five minutes until shallots turn translucent.

3. Add spices to the pan and combine well with garlic and shallots. Stir for two minutes.

4. Add the tomatoes to the pan and squash them using a spoon or spatula. Add four tbsps. of water to the pan and simmer for twelve minutes.

5. Add cooked chickpeas and mix well. Add pepper, sugar, and salt.

6. Serve the cooked chickpeas on bread slices.

Asparagus And Tomato Quiche

Total Prep & Cooking Time: One hour and twenty minutes

Yields. Eight servings

Nutrition Facts: Calories: 219 | Protein: 4.1g | Carbs: 20.6g | Fat: 11.7g | Fiber: 3g

Ingredients:

- Two cups of flour
- Half tsp. of salt
- Half cup of non-dairy butter
- Two tbsps. of water (ice cold)

For filling:

- One tbsp. of coconut oil
- One cup of asparagus (chopped)
- One-fourth cup of onion (minced)
- Three tbsps. of each
  - Sun-dried tomatoes (chopped)
  - Nutritional yeast
  - Basil (chopped)
- One block of tofu (firm)
- One tbsp. of each
  - Flour
  - Non-dairy milk
- One tsp. of each
  - Minced onion (dehydrated)
  - Mustard
- Two tsps. of lemon juice
- Half tsp. of each
  - Salt

- o   Turmeric
- o   Liquid smoke

Method:

1. Spray a pie pan with oil and keep aside. Preheat your oven at 180 degrees Celsius.

2. Mix salt along with flour in a bowl. Add non-dairy butter along with cold water to the flour. Knead the dough on a working surface.

3. Press the dough on the pan. Bake the dough in the preheated oven for ten minutes.

4. Heat some oil in a pan and start adding asparagus, tomato, and onion— Cook for three minutes.

5. Combine onion, tofu, yeast, flour, non-dairy milk, lemon juice, liquid smoke, and salt in a blender.

6. Combine the mixture of asparagus with the tofu mixture.

7. Add the filling on the baked crust and smoothen the top.

8. Bake for half an hour.

9. Serve warm.

Breakfast Bowl

Total Prep & Cooking Time: One hour and twenty-five minutes

Yields: Two servings

Nutrition Facts: Calories: 350 | Protein: 7.2g | Carbs: 54g | Fat: 11.3g | Fiber: 9.3g

Ingredients:

- Two small sweet potatoes
- Cinnamon (ground, according to taste)
- Two tbsps. of each
  - Chopped nuts
  - Raisins
  - Almond butter

Method:

1. Preheat your oven at 180/160 degrees Celsius. Wash the potatoes and dry them using a kitchen towel. Use a fork for poking holes in the potatoes and wrap them using aluminum foil. Bake the potatoes for eighty minutes. Allow the potatoes to cool down before peeling.

2. Peel the baked potatoes and mash them with cinnamon.

3. Top with chopped nuts and raisins. Drizzle some almond butter from the top and serve.

Tofu Pancakes

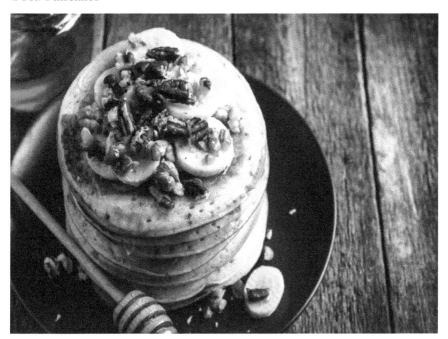

Total Prep & Cooking Time: Twenty minutes

Yields: Six servings

Nutrition Facts: Calories: 370 | Protein: 11.2g | Carbs: 46.3g | Fat: 13.2g | Fiber: 7.9g

Ingredients:

- Fifty grams of Brazil nuts
- Three bananas (sliced)
- Three-hundred grams of raspberries
- Maple syrup (for serving)

For batter:

- Four-hundred grams of firm tofu
- Two tsps. of each
    - Lemon juice
    - Vanilla extract
- Four-hundred ml of almond milk
- One tbsp. of vegetable oil
- Two cups of buckwheat flour
- Four tbsps. of sugar
- Two tsps. of mixed spice (ground)
- One tbsp. of baking powder

Method:

1. Preheat your oven at 160 degrees Celsius. Cook the nuts by scattering them in a tray for five minutes. Chop the nuts.

2. Add vanilla, tofu, almond milk, and lemon juice in a deep bowl; blend the mixture using a stick blender. Add oil to the mixture and blend again.

3. Take a large bowl and combine the dry ingredients; add one tsp. of salt and combine. Add the mixture of tofu and combine.

4. Heat a pan and add one tsp. oil in it. Make sure that the pan is not excessively hot.

5. Use a large spoon for dropping three spoons of batter in the pan. Swirl the pan for making the pancake even—Cook for two minutes on each side. Repeat the same for the remaining batter.

6. Serve with berries, bananas, nuts, and drizzle some maple syrup from the top.

Chapter 2: Side Dish Recipes

Side dish plays a profound role in any proper meal. I have included some tasty and easy vegan side dish recipes in this section.

Baked Beans
Total Prep & Cooking Time: Five hours and twenty minutes

Yields: Ten servings

Nutrition Facts: Calories: 249 | Protein: 11.2g | Carbs: 45.3g | Fat: 2.9g | Fiber: 13.7g

Ingredients:

- Sixteen ounces of navy beans (dry)
- Six cups of water
- Two tbsps. of olive oil
- Two cups of sweet onion (chopped)
- One garlic clove (minced)
- Four cans of tomato sauce
- One-fourth cup of brown sugar
- Half cup of molasses
- Three tbsps. of cider vinegar
- Three bay leaves
- One tsp. of mustard (dry)
- One-fourth tsp. of each
  - Black pepper (ground)
  - Nutmeg (ground)
  - Cinnamon (ground)

Method:

1. Add water and beans in a pot and boil the mixture. Lower the flame and cook for one hour. Cook until the beans are tender. Drain the beans and keep aside.

2. Preheat your oven to 160 degrees Celsius.

3. Take an iron skillet and heat oil in it. Add onions in the oil. Cook for two minutes. Add garlic to the pan.

4. Combine the onion mixture with the cooked beans. Add tomato sauce, molasses, vinegar, brown sugar, pepper, bay leaves, cinnamon, mustard, and nutmeg. Mix well.

5. Cover the dish and bake for three hours. Stir in between.

6. Remove the cover and bake for forty minutes.

Baked Potato Wedges

Total Prep & Cooking Time: Fifty-five minutes

Yields: Four servings

Nutrition Facts: Calories: 234 | Protein: 5.1g | Carbs: 42.6g | Fat: 4.3g | Fiber: 8.9g

Ingredients:

- One tbsp. of olive oil
- Eight sweet potatoes (sliced into quarters)
- Half tsp. of paprika

Method:

1. Preheat your oven at 160/180 degrees Celsius.

2. Grease a baking sheet with cooking spray.

3. Combine potatoes and paprika in a bowl. Add the potatoes to the baking sheet.

4. Bake for forty minutes.

5. Serve warm.

Black Beans And Quinoa

Total Prep & Cooking Time: Fifty minutes

Yields: Ten servings

Nutrition Facts: Calories: 143 | Protein: 8.7g | Carbs: 25.6g | Fat: 1.2g | Fiber: 8.7g

Ingredients:

- One tsp. of vegetable oil
- One large onion (chopped)
- Three garlic cloves (chopped)
- Three-fourth cup of quinoa
- Two cups of vegetable stock
- One tsp. of cumin (ground)
- One-fourth tsp. of cayenne powder
- One cup of corn kernels (frozen)
- Two cans of black beans (rinsed)
- Half cup of cilantro (chopped)
- Pepper and salt (according to taste)

Method:

1. Take a medium pan and heat oil in it. Add garlic and onion to the pan. Cook for ten minutes until browned.

2. Add quinoa to the pan and mix well. Cover the mixture with vegetable stock. Season with salt, pepper, and cayenne. Boil the mixture. Cover the pan and simmer for twenty minutes until quinoa gets tender.

3. Add the corn kernels to the pan and simmer for five minutes.

4. Add cilantro and black beans to the mixture.

5. Serve hot.

Roasted Lemon Garlic Broccoli

Total Prep & Cooking Time: Twenty-five minutes

Yields: Six servings

Nutrition Facts: Calories: 48.3 | Protein: 3g | Carbs: 6.9g | Fat: 1.8g | Fiber: 3g

Ingredients:

- Two heads of broccoli (separate the florets)
- Two tsps. of olive oil (extra virgin)
- One tsp. of salt
- Half tsp. of black pepper (ground)
- One garlic clove (minced)
- One-fourth tsp. of lemon juice

Method:

1. Preheat your oven at 180/200 degrees Celsius.

2. Toss the florets of broccoli with olive oil in a bowl. Add pepper, garlic, and salt. Spread the coated broccoli florets on a baking sheet.

3. Bake for twenty minutes.

4. Add lemon juice from the top and serve warm.

Spicy Tofu
Total Prep & Cooking Time: Twenty minutes

Yields: Four servings

Nutrition Facts: Calories: 305.2 | Protein: 20.1g | Carbs: 15.4g | Fat: 19.3g | Fiber: 5.2g

Ingredients:

- Three tbsps. of peanut oil
- One red onion (sliced)
- One pound of tofu (firm, cubed)
- One bell pepper (sliced)
- One chili pepper (chopped)
- Three garlic cloves (crushed)
- One-third cup of hot water
- Two tbsps. of each
  - Soy sauce
  - White vinegar
- One tsp. of cornstarch
- One tbsp. of each
  - Red pepper flakes (crushed)
  - Brown sugar

Method:

1. Take a wok and heat oil in it. Add the tofu to the oil and keep cooking until browned. Add bell pepper, onion, garlic, and chili pepper. Mix well and cook for five minutes.

2. Whisk vinegar, soy sauce, red pepper flakes, brown sugar, and cornstarch in a bowl.

3. Add the mixture of vinegar to the wok and toss well for coating. Simmer the mixture for five minutes.

4. Serve hot.

Spanish Rice

Total Prep & Cooking Time: Forty minutes

Yields: Four servings

Nutrition Facts: Calories: 267.2 | Protein: 4.7g | Carbs: 42.7g | Fat: 5.6g | Fiber: 3g

Ingredients:

- Two tbsps. of vegetable oil
- One cup of white rice (uncooked)
- One onion (chopped)
- Half bell pepper (chopped)
- Two cups of water
- One can of green chilies and diced tomatoes
- Two tsps. of chili powder
- One tsp. of salt

Method:

1. Take a deep skillet and heat oil in it. Add onion, rice, and bell pepper to the skillet. Sauté until onions are soft and rice gets browned.

2. Add tomatoes and water to the skillet. Add salt and chili powder.

3. Simmer the mixture for thirty minutes and cover the skillet.

4. Serve hot.

Pepper And Lemon Pasta

Total Prep & Cooking Time: Twenty minutes

Yields: Eight servings

Nutrition Facts: Calories: 232.8 | Protein: 8.5g | Carbs: 41g | Fat: 4.6g | Fiber: 3.6g

Ingredients:

- One pound of spaghetti
- Two tbsps. of olive oil
- One tbsp. of basil (dried)
  Three tbsps. of lemon juice
- Black pepper (ground, according to taste)

Method:

1. Take a large pot and boil water in it with light salt. Add the pasta to the pot and cook for ten minutes. Drain the pasta.

2. Combine lemon juice, black pepper, lemon juice, and basil in a bowl.

3. Add the lemon mixture to the cooked pasta and toss it properly.

4. Serve cold or hot.

Chapter 3: High Protein Recipes

The vegan diet is rich in proteins, as it is mainly composed of plant compounds. Here are some easy to make vegan high protein recipes for you.

Kale Salad With Spicy Tempeh Bits And Chickpeas

Total Prep & Cooking Time: Forty-five minutes

Yields: Four servings

Nutrition Facts: Calories: 473 | Protein: 25g | Carbs: 41g | Fat: 27.1g | Fiber: 17.3g

Ingredients:

- Eight ounces of tempeh
- One-fourth cup of vegetable oil
- One-fourth tsp. of salt
- Two tsps. of each
  - Garlic powder
  - Onion powder
  - Sweet paprika
- One tsp. of each
  - Lemon pepper
  - Chili powder
- One-eighth tsp. of cayenne powder

For salad:

- 400 grams of kale (chopped)
- One cup of carrots (shredded)
- One can of chickpeas
- Two tbsps. of sesame seeds

For dressing:

- Half cup of rice vinegar

- One-fourth cup of soy sauce

- Two tbsps. of sesame oil

- One tbsp. of ginger (grated)

Method:

1. Boil water with salt in a large pot. Blanch the kale for thirty seconds. Wash blanched kale under running water. Squeeze out excess water from kale and keep aside.

2. Preheat your oven to 180 degrees Celsius.

3. Mix all the spices for tempeh in a mixing bowl.

4. Cut tempeh into very thin slices.

5. Dip each tempeh slice in oil and arrange them on a baking sheet. Line the tray using parchment paper. Sprinkle the mix of spices from the top. Coat well.

6. Bake tempeh for twenty minutes until crispy and brown in color.

7. Take a large bowl and combine the listed ingredients for the salad.

8. Combine the ingredients of dressing in a jar and shake well.

9. Pour the dressing over the prepared salad. Toss well. Make sure the salad gets coated properly with the dressing.

10. Crumble the slices of tempeh over the salad.

Protein Bars

Total Prep & Cooking Time: One hour and twenty minutes

Yields: Ten servings

Nutrition Facts: Calories: 292 | Protein: 13g | Carbs: 37.9g | Fat: 9.6g | Fiber: 2.3g

Ingredients:

For crust:

- Two cups of oat flour
- Six apricots (dried)
- One-fourth cup of each
  - Brown rice syrup
  - Cocoa powder

For layer:

- One cup of oat flour
- Half cup of each
  - Vegan protein powder (chocolate)
  - Rolled oats
- One-fourth tsp. of salt
- Two tbsps. of each
  - Hemp seeds (hulled)
  - Chia seeds
- Half cup of almond butter

- One-fourth cup of any vegan sweetener
- One cup of coconut milk
- One tbsp. flax seeds (ground)

Method:

1. Combine all the ingredients for the crust in a blender. Keep the dough aside.

2. Take a large bowl and mix the dry ingredients for the next layer. You can use a fork for proper mixing.

3. Mix water and flax in a bowl and keep aside until it turns into a gel.

4. Add almond butter, sweetener, coconut milk, and flax gel to the mixture of dry ingredients. Use a fork for mixing properly.

5. Pour the mixture in a food processor and blend well for making it smooth.

6. Use parchment paper for lining a baking sheet. Add the crust to the sheet and press the crust out. Add the next layer on the crust and evenly spread it out.

7. Put the baking sheet in the freezer for one hour.

8. Serve by cutting bars of your desired size and shape.

Tofu And Spinach Scramble

Total Prep & Cooking Time: Thirty minutes

Yields: Two servings

Nutrition Facts: Calories: 319 | Protein: 22.1g | Carbs: 11.4g | Fat: 22g | Fiber: 6.5g

Ingredients:

- Fourteen ounces of tofu (firm, cut into cubes of half-inch)
- Half tsp. of turmeric (ground)
- Black pepper and kosher salt (to taste)
- One-eighth tsp. of cayenne powder (ground)
- Two tbsps. of olive oil (extra virgin)
- Three scallions (sliced)
- Five ounces of spinach (chopped)
- Two tsps. of lemon juice
- One cup of grape tomatoes (halved)
- Half cup of basil (chopped)

Method:

1. Mix turmeric, tofu, one-fourth tsp. of salt, cayenne, and half tsp. of black pepper in a bowl. Toss the ingredients for mixing properly.

2. Take a large skillet and heat oil in it; add the scallions and stir for about one minute. Add tofu mixture and cook for five minutes until the tofu gets browned.

3. Add lemon juice, spinach, and half tsp. of salt to the tofu. Cook for one minute until the spinach wilts. Add tomatoes and stir for one minute.

4. Remove the skillet from heat and add basil.

5. Serve hot.

Vegan Tacos

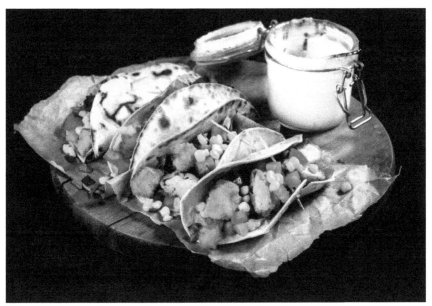

Total Prep & Cooking Time: Twenty minutes

Yields: Six servings

Nutrition Facts: Calories: 402 | Protein: 29g | Carbs: 71.2g | Fat: 5.4g | Fiber: 20.3g

Ingredients:

- One tsp. of vegetable oil
- Half onion (diced)
- Two tsps. of jalapeno (chopped)
- Twelve ounces of soy chorizo (remove the casing)

- Sixteen ounces of refried black beans
- Twelve tortillas (corn)
- Cilantro (chopped)

Method:

1. Take a skillet and heat oil in it. Add onion and jalapeno to the skillet—Cook for ten minutes. Add chorizo and cook for five minutes.

2. Take a small pan and cook the beans on low heat.

3. Arrange two tortillas for making six tacos in total.

4. Spread the beans on the tortillas; top the beans with the mixture of chorizo. Serve with cilantro from the top.

Grilled Tofu Steaks And Spinach Salad

Total Prep & Cooking Time: One hour

Yields: Two servings

Nutrition Facts: Calories: 154 | Protein: 22g | Carbs: 8g | Fat: 11.3g | Fiber: 9.3g

Ingredients:

For tofu steak:

- Half block of tofu (firm)
- One tbsp. of soy sauce
- One tsp. of each
  - Miso paste

- o Tomato paste
- o Olive oil
- Half tsp. of maple syrup
- One-fourth cup of breadcrumbs

For spinach salad:

- Two cups of baby spinach
- One tbsp. of each
  - o Olive oil (extra virgin)
  - o Pine nuts
  - o Lemon juice
- Pinch of salt
- Pinch of black pepper (ground)

Method:

1. Cut the tofu block in half and squeeze out any excess water. Make sure you do not break the block of tofu. Use paper towels for drying the tofu.

2. Cut the tofu in size and shape of your choice.

3. Take a small mixing bowl and combine tomato paste, soy sauce, olive oil, sesame, miso paste, and maple syrup. Mix until the sauce is smooth.

4. Spread breadcrumbs in a shallow dish.

5. Dip the pieces of tofu in the prepared sauce and then coat them in breadcrumbs. Repeat for the remaining tofu.

6. Grease a grill pan with some olive oil. Add the tofu steaks and cook for fifteen minutes on each side. Cook until both sides are browned.

7. For the salad, mix the listed ingredients in a medium-sized mixing bowl. Toss the ingredients properly.

8. Serve the tofu steaks with spinach salad by the side.

Corn, Quinoa, And Edamame Salad

Total Prep & Cooking Time: Two hours and ten minutes

Yields: Four servings

Nutrition Facts: Calories: 130 | Protein: 18g | Carbs: 13g | Fat: 5.8g | Fiber: 3.1g

Ingredients:

- One cup of corn kernels (frozen)
- Two cups of shelled edamame
- Half cup of cooked quinoa
- One green onion (sliced)
- Half sweet bell pepper (diced)
- Two tbsps. of cilantro (chopped)
- One and a half tbsps. of olive oil
- One tbsp. of each
    - Lime juice
    - Lemon juice
- One-fourth tsp. of each
    - Salt
    - Thyme (dried)
    - Chili powder
    - Black pepper (ground)

Method:

1. Boil corn and edamame in water with a little bit of salt. Drain and keep aside.

2. Take a bowl and mix corn, edamame, quinoa, bell pepper, green onion, and cilantro.

3. Whisk together lemon juice, olive oil, lime juice, chili powder, salt, thyme, and black pepper in a small bowl.

4. Pour the dressing all over the salad. Mix well.

5. Chill in the refrigerator for two hours.

Lentil Soup

Total Prep & Cooking Time: Fifty-five minutes

Yields: Six servings

Nutrition Facts: Calories: 230 | Protein: 9.2g | Carbs: 31.2g | Fat: 8.6g | Fiber: 11.3g

Ingredients:

- Two tbsps. of olive oil (extra virgin)
- One onion (diced)

- Two carrots (diced)
- Two stalks of celery (diced)
- One bell pepper (diced)
- Three garlic cloves (minced)
- One tbsp. of cumin
- One-fourth tsp. of paprika
- One tsp. of oregano
- Two cups of tomatoes (diced)
- Two cans of green lentils (rinsed)
- Eight cups of vegetable stock
- Half tsp. of salt
- Cilantro (for garnishing)
- One ripe avocado (diced)

Method:

1. Heat some oil in a pot. Start adding bell pepper, onion, carrots, and celery to the pot. Sauté the veggies for five minutes until tender; add paprika, cumin, garlic, and oregano. Mix well.

2. Add chilies, tomatoes, stock, salt, and lentils; simmer the mixture for forty minutes. Add pepper and salt according to taste.

3. Serve with avocado and cilantro from the top.

Chapter 4: Dessert Recipes

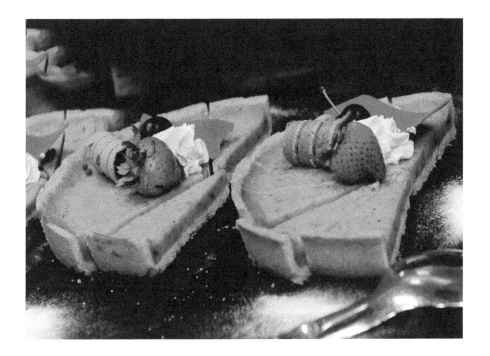

Everyone loves to have some dessert after having their meals. Desserts can be vegan too. So in this section, I have included some tasty dessert recipes that you can make easily.

Chocolate Pudding

Total Prep & Cooking Time: Forty-five minutes

Yields: Two servings

Nutrition Facts: Calories: 265.1 | Protein: 8.3g | Carbs: 52.2g | Fat: 4.6g | Fiber:

4.9g

Ingredients:

- Three tbsps. of cornstarch
- Two tbsps. of water
- Two cups of soy milk
- One-fourth tsp. of vanilla extract
- One-fourth cup of white sugar
- One cup of cocoa powder

Method:

1. Take a small bowl and mix water and cornstarch for forming a fine paste.

2. Take a saucepan and heat it over medium flame. Add soy milk, sugar, vanilla, a mixture of cornstarch, and cocoa. Stir the mixture until it starts boiling. Keep cooking until the mixture gets thick.

3. Allow the pudding to cool for five minutes.

4. Chill in the fridge for twenty minutes.

Orange Cake

Total Prep & Cooking Time: Forty-five minutes

Yields: Sixteen servings

Nutrition Facts: Calories: 147.3 | Protein: 1.9g | Carbs: 21.6g | Fat: 6.3g | Fiber: 0.8g

Ingredients:

- One large-sized onion (peeled)
- Two cups of flour
- One cup of white sugar
- Half cup of vegetable oil
- One and a half tsps. of baking soda
- Half tsp. of salt

Method:

1. Preheat your oven to 190 degrees Celsius. Grease a baking pan with some oil.

2. Blend the orange in a food processor until it gets completely liquefied.

3. Combine orange juice, sugar, flour, vegetable oil, baking soda, and salt. Pour the cake batter into prepared baking pan.

4. Bake the cake for thirty minutes.

Notes:

- In case you do not want to make orange juice at home, you can use orange juice from the store.

- This cake can be converted into a plain cake by omitting orange juice and using soy milk along with rice milk.

Pumpkin Tofu Pie

Total Prep & Cooking Time: Two hours

Yields: Eight servings

Nutrition Facts: Calories: 229.3 | Protein: 4.7g | Carbs: 33.6g | Fat: 8.6g | Fiber: 3.7g

Ingredients

- Ten ounces of silken tofu (drained)
- One can of pumpkin puree
- Three-fourth cup of white sugar
- Half tsp. of salt
- One tsp. of cinnamon (ground)
- One-fourth tsp. of ginger (ground)
- One-eighth tsp. of cloves (ground)
- One pie crust (unbaked)

Method:

1. Preheat the oven at 220/230 degrees Celsius.

2. Add pumpkin puree, tofu, cinnamon, salt, sugar, clove, and ginger in a food processor. Blend the ingredients until smooth.

3. Pour over the blended mixture into the crust.

4. Bake the pie for fifteen minutes and then reduce the temperature to 175 degrees Celsius. Bake again for forty minutes.

5. Let the pie cool down.

6. Serve at room temperature.

Note: If you are allergic to certain ingredients, check the ingredients of the pie crust.

Vegan Brownie

Total Prep & Cooking Time: Fifty minutes

Yields: Sixteen servings

Nutrition Facts: Calories: 254.3 | Protein: 2.6g | Carbs: 38.3g | Fat: 13.6g | Fiber: 2.8g

Ingredients:

- Two cups of flour
- Two cups of white sugar
- Three-fourth cup of cocoa powder (unsweetened)
- One tsp. of baking powder
- Half tsp. of salt
- One cup of each
  - Vegetable oil
  - Water
- One and a half tsps. of vanilla extract

Method:

1. Preheat your oven at 160/175 degrees Celsius.

2. Take a large bowl and combine sugar, flour, cocoa powder, salt, and baking powder. Add vegetable oil, vanilla extract, and water to the mixture. Mix well for making a smooth batter.

3. Spread the brownie mix in a baking pan.

4. Bake the brownie for thirty minutes.

5. Allow the brownie to cool for ten minutes.

6. Cut in squares and serve.

Vegan Cupcake

Total Prep & Cooking Time: Twenty-five minutes

Yields: Eighteen servings

Nutrition Facts: Calories: 150.2 | Protein: 1.9g | Carbs: 21.6g | Fat: 6.3g | Fiber: 0.9g

Ingredients:

- One tbsp. of cider vinegar
- Two cups of almond milk
- Two and a half cups of flour
- One cup of white sugar
- Two tsps. of baking powder
- Half tsp. of each
    - Salt
    - Baking soda
    - Coconut oil (warmed)
- One and a half tsps. of vanilla extract

Method:

1. Preheat the oven at 160/175 degrees Celsius. Grease eighteen muffin cups using some oil.

2. Mix cider vinegar and almond milk in a bowl. Allow it to stand for five minutes until the mixture gets curdled.

3. Take a bowl and combine sugar, salt, baking powder, flour, and baking soda.

4. Take another bowl and combine coconut oil, vanilla, and almond milk mixture. Add this mixture to the mixture of dry ingredients.

5. Divide the batter into muffin cups—Bake for twenty minutes.

6. Allow the cupcakes to sit for ten minutes.

7. Serve with the desired frosting from the top.

Vanilla Cake

Total Prep & Cooking Time: Fifty minutes

Yields: Eight servings

Nutrition Facts: Calories: 277.9 | Protein: 3.5g | Carbs: 44.2g | Fat: 9.2g | Fiber: 0.9g

Ingredients:

- One cup of soy milk
- One tbsp. of apple cider vinegar
- One and a half cup of flour
- One cup of white sugar
- One tsp. of each
    - Baking powder
    - Baking soda
- Half tsp. of salt
- One-third cup of canola oil
- One-fourth tsp. of almond extract
- One tbsp. of vanilla extract
- One-fourth cup of water

Method:

1. Preheat your oven at about 160/175 degrees Celsius. Grease a baking pan with some oil.

2. Mix vinegar and soy milk in a large cup.

3. Combine sugar, flour, salt, baking soda, and baking powder in a bowl.

4. Add lemon juice, canola oil, vanilla extract, almond extract, and water to the mixture of soy milk. Stir the mixture of soy milk into the mixture of flour. Mix well until there is no lump.

5. Pour the cake batter in the baking dish.

6. Bake in the preheated oven for thirty-five minutes.

Miracle Fudge

Total Prep & Cooking Time: One hour and ten minutes

Yields: Twenty-four servings

Nutrition Facts: Calories: 77.3 | Protein: 0.9g | Carbs: 4.9g | Fat: 6.2g | Fiber: 1.2g

Ingredients:

- Half cup of cocoa (unsweetened)
- One cup of maple syrup
- One tsp. of vanilla extract
- One pinch of salt
- One-third cup of each
  - Chopped walnuts
  - Coconut oil (melted)
- One tsp. of cocoa powder (unsweetened, for dusting)

Method:

1. Add half cup of cocoa powder in a bowl along with maple syrup; give it a stir. Add vanilla extract and salt. Add melted coconut oil and combine well.

2. Add walnuts in a pan and toast them for one minute.

3. Add the toasted walnuts to the fudge. Mix well.

4. Pour the mixture of fudge into a silicone mold. Smoothen the top.

5. Wrap the silicone mold using plastic wrap and put it in the freezer for thirty minutes. Take out the fudge pieces from the mold and dust with cocoa powder from the top.

6. Serve cold.

Chapter 5: Sauces & Dips Recipes

Sauces and dips are important components of any meal that can make the food tastier. Here are some vegan sauces and dips recipes for you.

Tomato Jam
Total Prep & Cooking Time: Forty-five minutes

Yields: One full cup

Nutrition Facts: Calories: 34 | Protein: 0.2g | Carbs: 8.6g | Fat: 0.1g | Fiber: 0.2g

Ingredients:

- Two pounds of plum tomatoes
- One-fourth cup of coconut sugar
- Half tsp. of salt
- One-fourth tsp. of paprika
- One tsp. of vinegar (white wine)
- Black pepper (to taste)

Method:

1. Take a large pot and boil water in it; add the tomatoes to the water and boil for one minute. Remove the tomatoes and put them in an ice-water bath.

2. Peel the blanched tomatoes and chop them.

3. Add chopped tomatoes in a pot over a medium flame. Add sugar and stir the mixture—Cook for ten minutes.

4. Add pepper, salt, and paprika. Simmer for ten minutes until the jam thickens.

5. Remove from heat and add white wine vinegar. Serve with crackers, burgers, toasts, etc.

Walnut Kale Pesto

Total Prep & Cooking Time: Thirty minutes

Yields: One small bowl

Nutrition Facts: Calories: 240 | Protein: 3.6g | Carbs: 2.6g | Fat: 22.3g | Fiber: 0.8g

Ingredients:

- Half bunch of kale (chopped)
- Half cup of walnuts (chopped)
- Two garlic cloves (minced)
- One-fourth cup of yeast
- One cup of olive oil
- Three tbsps. of lemon juice
- Pepper and salt (for seasoning)

Method:

1. Take a pot and boil water in it. Add kale to the pot with one tsp. of salt— Cook for five minutes.

2. Add kale, garlic, walnuts, olive oil, yeast, along with lemon juice in a food processor. Add pepper and salt according to your taste. Blend well.

Ranch Dressing

Total Prep & Cooking Time: Thirty minutes

Yields: One small bowl

Nutrition Facts: Calories: 92 | Protein: 0.1g | Carbs: 1g | Fat: 9.1g | Fiber: 0.4g

Ingredients:

- One cup of vegan mayo
- Half tsp. of each
  - Onion powder
  - Garlic powder
- One-fourth tsp. of black pepper (ground)
- Two tsps. of parsley (chopped)
- One tbsp. of dill (chopped)
- Half cup of soy milk (unsweetened)

Method:

1. Mix the listed ingredients in a medium mixing bowl.

2. If you want the dressing to be thin, add a bit of almond milk. Allow the dressing to sit for a few minutes.

3. Chill the prepared dressing.

Notes:

- You can serve the dressing with any savory snacks, sandwiches, quick-bites, salads, etc.

- You can store the leftover dressing in the fridge for two days.

- You can add some ground nuts for enhancing the flavor

PART III

Vegetarian Cookbook

The vegetarian diet has gained immense popularity in the last few years. According to some studies, it has been found that an estimated 18% of the world population is vegetarian. Apart from all the environmental and ethical benefits of removing meat from the diet, a properly planned vegetarian diet can reduce the risk of various chronic diseases, improve diet quality, and help in losing weight. The vegetarian diet also does not include poultry and fish. The majority of the people opt for a vegetarian diet for personal or religious reasons and for ethical reasons, such as animal rights. Other people opt for it for various environmental reasons, like livestock production, which results in the emission of greenhouse gases.

A vegetarian diet comes along with a wide array of benefits. It has been found that vegetarians have a better quality of diet when compared to meat-eaters. They also have a higher intake of beneficial nutrients, such as vitamin C, fiber, magnesium, and vitamin E. Switching from a normal meat diet to a vegetarian diet can result to be an effective strategy in case you want to lose weight. For instance, in a review of twelve studies, it has been found that vegetarians can lose about four pounds of weight over eighteen weeks than non-vegetarians. Also, vegetarians have lower BMI or body mass index than non-vegetarians.

Some research found that a vegetarian diet can be linked to a lower risk of developing cancer and those of the colon, breast, stomach, and rectum. However, it lacks enough evidence to prove that a vegetarian diet can effectively reduce cancer risk. People who follow a vegetarian diet can maintain healthy levels of blood sugar. It can also help in preventing the onset of diabetes by controlling the levels of blood sugar. Vegetarian diets help in the reduction of various heart diseases that can make your heart stronger and healthier.

A vegetarian diet needs to include a wide mixture of veggies, fruits, healthy fats, grains, and proteins. To replace the protein that you get from meat in a diet, you will need to include plant foods rich in proteins such as seeds, nuts, legumes, seitan, tofu, and tempeh. Consuming whole foods rich in nutrients, such as vegetables and fruits, can provide your body with the necessary minerals and vitamins to fill the nutritional gaps in a diet. Some of the food items that you can include in your diet are:

- **Fruits:** Bananas, apples, melons, oranges, peaches, pears

- **Vegetables:** Asparagus, leafy greens, carrots, broccoli

- **Legumes:** Beans, lentils, chickpeas, peas

- **Seeds:** Chia, flaxseed, hemp

- **Nuts:** Walnuts, cashews, almonds

- **Proteins:** Seitan, natto, tofu, eggs, tempeh

You cannot include food items such as fish, seafood, meat, poultry, and ingredients that are based on meat. Restriction of eggs and dairy products are applicable for the vegans and not for vegetarians. I have included some tasty and easy vegetarian recipes that will help you to plan your diet effectively.

Chapter 1: Breakfast Recipes

No matter which diet you follow, breakfast is very important in all cases. In this section, you will find some easy-to-make and tasty breakfast recipes that you can include in your vegetarian diet.

Black Bean Bowl

Total Prep & Cooking Time: Fifteen minutes

Yields: Two servings

Nutrition Facts: Calories: 620.1 | Protein: 28.9g | Carbs: 47.6g | Fat: 37.1g | Fiber: 23.2g

Ingredients:

- Two tbsps. of olive oil
- Four eggs (beaten)

- One can of black beans (rinsed)
- One avocado (sliced)
- One-fourth cup of salsa
- One tsp. of each
  - Black pepper (ground)
  - Salt

Method:

1. Take a small pan and heat oil in it. Add the eggs and scramble for five minutes.

2. Place the beans in a bowl. Heat the beans in the oven for one minute.

3. Divide the beans into two serving bowls.

4. Top the beans with scrambled eggs, salsa, and avocado. Add pepper and salt according to taste.

Coconut Blueberry Ricotta Bowl

Total Prep & Cooking Time: Twenty minutes

Yields: One serving

Nutrition Facts: Calories: 303.2 | Protein: 9.5g | Carbs: 32.1g | Fat: 15.3g | Fiber: 3.9g

Ingredients:

- One-fourth cup of ricotta cheese
- One tbsp. of each
    - Honey
    - Coconut milk
    - Slivered almonds
    - Coconut flakes
- Half cup of blueberries

Method:

1. Combine coconut milk and ricotta in a medium-sized bowl. Drizzle honey from the top and add coconut and almonds.

2. Serve with blueberries from the top.

Broccoli Quiche
Total Prep & Cooking Time: Fifty minutes

Yields: Six servings

Nutrition Facts: Calories: 378.2 | Protein: 17.3g | Carbs: 21.1g | Fat: 25.8g |
Fiber: 3.1g

Ingredients:

- One pie crust (unbaked)
- Three tbsps. of butter
- One onion (minced)
- One tsp. of each
    - Garlic (minced)
    - Salt
- Two cups of broccoli (chopped)
- One and a half cup of mozzarella cheese (shredded)
- Four eggs (beaten)
- Two and a half cup of milk
- Half tsp. of black pepper
- One tbsp. of butter (melted)

Method:

1. Start by preheating your oven at 175 degrees Celsius. Use pie crust for lining a deep pie pan.

2. Take a large saucepan and add butter to it. Add broccoli, onion, and garlic. Cook the veggies slowly until tender. Add the cooked veggies to the pie crust and add cheese from the top.

3. Mix milk and eggs in a bowl; add pepper and salt for seasoning. Add the remaining butter to the milk mixture. Pour the mixture over the mixture of vegetables.

4. Bake the quiche in the oven for forty minutes or until the center has properly set.

Tomato Bagel Sandwich

Total Prep & Cooking Time: Twenty minutes

Yields: One serving

Nutrition Facts: Calories: 346.3 | Protein: 13.1g | Carbs: 48.6g | Fat: 10.7g | Fiber: 2.9g

Ingredients:

- One bagel (split, toasted)
- Two tbsps. of cream cheese
- One large tomato (sliced thinly)
- Pepper and salt (to season)
- Four basil leaves

Method:

1. Spread the cream cheese on the halves of the bagel.

2. Top the cheese layer with slices of tomato. Add pepper and salt for seasoning.

3. Serve with basil leaves from the top.

Cornmeal And Blueberry Pancakes

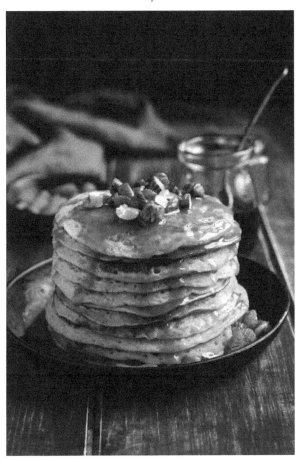

Total Prep & Cooking Time: Thirty minutes

Yields: Six servings

Nutrition Facts: Calories: 180.3 | Protein: 5.2g | Carbs: 26.8g | Fat: 5.1g | Fiber: 4.6g

Ingredients:

- One cup of soy milk
- Half cup of each
    - Water
    - Cornmeal (ground)
- One and a half cup of wheat flour
- One tsp. baking powder
- One-third tsp. baking soda
- One-fourth tsp. of salt
- One cup of blueberries
- Two tbsps. of vegetable oil

Method:

1. Preheat your oven at 95 degrees Celsius.

2. Combine water and soy milk in a bowl.

3. Take a large mixing bowl and combine cornmeal, baking soda, flour, salt, and baking powder. Add the mixture of soy milk. Combine properly. Add the blueberries and allow the batter to rest for five minutes.

4. Take a large skillet and grease it using oil. Add one-fourth cup of the batter in the skillet. Cook until the pancakes are bubbly on the top, and the edges are dry. Cook for five minutes on each side. Repeat with the remaining batter.

5. Serve hot with jam or syrup.

Breakfast Tortilla

Total Prep & Cooking Time: Twenty minutes

Yields: Two servings

Nutrition Facts: Calories: 381.3 | Protein: 15.8g | Carbs: 38.1g | Fat: 18.7g | Fiber: 4.5g

Ingredients:

- Two tbsps. of beans (refried)
- Three tbsps. of salsa
- Three large eggs (beaten)
- One tbsp. of mayonnaise
- Four tortillas (flour)
- One and a half cup of lettuce (shredded)

Method:

1. Combine salsa and beans in a small bowl.

2. Take an iron skillet and heat oil in it. Add the eggs and let the bottom set—Cook for one minute. Spread the mixture of beans on half of the egg and flip one side for making the shape of a half-circle. Cook until the eggs set properly.

3. Spread mayonnaise on the tortillas.

4. Cut the cooked eggs into four equal pieces. Place each piece of eggs on the tortillas. Top with lettuce.

5. Roll the tortillas. Serve hot.

Zucchini Frittata

Total Prep & Cooking Time: Forty minutes

Yields: Five servings

Nutrition Facts: Calories: 258.3 | Protein: 14.2g | Carbs: 9.1g | Fat: 19.6g | Fiber: 3.4g

Ingredients:

- One cup of water
- Three tbsps. of olive oil
- Half tsp. of salt
- Half bell pepper (green, chopped)
- Three zucchinis (cut in slices of half-inch)
- Two garlic cloves (peeled)
- One onion (diced)
- Six mushrooms (chopped)
- One tbsp. of butter
- Five eggs
- Pepper and salt (to taste)
- One and a half cup of mozzarella cheese (shredded)
- Three tbsps. of parmesan cheese

Method:

1. Start by preheating your oven at 160/175 degrees Celsius.

2. Take a large skillet and combine olive oil, water, green pepper, salt, garlic cloves, and zucchini. Simmer the mixture until the zucchini is soft— Cook for seven minutes.

3. Drain the water and remove the garlic; add mushroom, onion, and butter. Keep cooking until the onion turns transparent. Add the eggs and keep stirring. Add pepper and salt for seasoning. Cook until the eggs are firm.

4. Add mozzarella cheese from the top.

5. Bake in the oven for ten minutes.

6. Remove the frittata from the oven and add parmesan cheese from the top. Place under the broiler for about five minutes.

7. Cut the frittata in wedges and serve warm.

Oatmeal And Strawberry Smoothie

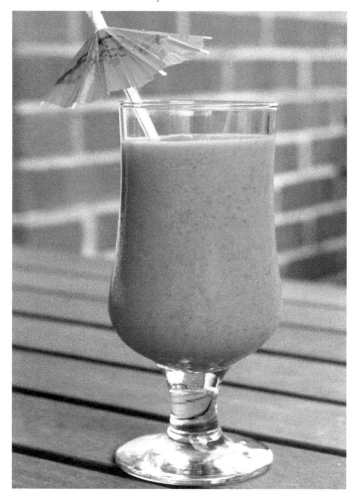

Total Prep & Cooking Time: Twenty minutes

Yields: Two servings

Nutrition Facts: Calories: 204.1 | Protein: 5.2g | Carbs: 41.3g | Fat: 2.7g | Fiber: 6.9g

Ingredients:

- One cup of almond milk
- Half cup of rolled oats
- Fourteen strawberries (frozen)
- One banana (cut in chunks)
- Two tsps. of agave nectar
- Half tsp. of vanilla extract

Method:

1. Add almond milk, strawberries, oats, agave nectar, banana, and vanilla extract in a food processor. Keep blending until smooth.

2. Serve with pieces of strawberry from the top.

Chapter 2: Appetizers Recipes

Hosting a party but not sure which appetizers to prepare as most of your guests are vegetarians? No worries as I have included some great vegetarian recipes for appetizers in this section.

Buffalo Cauliflower
Total Prep & Cooking Time: Thirty minutes

Yields: Twelve servings

Nutrition Facts: Calories: 120 | Protein: 4.2g | Carbs: 7.9g | Fat: 8.7g | Fiber: 2.3g

Ingredients

- One serving of cooking spray
- Half cup of buffalo sauce
- Three tbsps. of mayonnaise
- One large egg
- Six cups of cauliflower florets
- Two cups of garlic croutons
- One-fourth cup of parmesan cheese (grated)

For the dipping sauce:

- One-fourth cup of each
  - Sour cream
  - Blue cheese salad dressing
- One tsp. of black pepper (ground)

Method:

1. Start by preheating your oven to 230 degrees Celsius. Use a cooking spray for greasing a baking tray.

2. Combine mayonnaise, buffalo sauce, and egg in a bowl. Toss the florets of cauliflower in the mixture of sauce and coat properly.

3. Spread the tossed florets on the baking tray.

4. Add the croutons on a blender and pulse them into crumbs. Add the cheese and pulse again. Spread the mixture of cheese and croutons over the florets of cauliflower.

5. Bake for fifteen minutes until tender and browned. Allow the florets to sit for five minutes.

6. Mix all the ingredients for the dipping sauce.

7. Serve cauliflower florets with dip sauce by the side.

Garlic Bread And Veggie Delight

Total Prep & Cooking Time: Thirty minutes

Yields: Five servings

Nutrition Facts: Calories: 390.2 | Protein: 12.4g | Carbs: 58.7g | Fat: 11.6g | Fiber: 7.2g

Ingredients:

- One cup of olive oil
- One garlic clove (chopped)
- One eggplant (cubed)
- One zucchini (cubed)
- One tomato (chopped)
- One tsp. of salt
- Two tsps. of each
    - Basil (minced)
    - Oregano (minced)
- One baguette
- Four tsps. of garlic powder
- Six tsps. of butter

Method:

1. Take a large skillet and add olive oil to it. Add garlic and fry for two minutes until browned.

2. Add the zucchini and eggplant to the skillet and cook for five minutes. Make sure that the eggplant is tender and brown.

3. Add the chunks of tomato and combine the veggies; add basil, oregano, and salt. Cook for two minutes and remove from heat.

4. Preheat oven 140/165 degrees Celsius.

5. Slice the baguette into one-inch slices, approximately twelve slices. Add butter and garlic powder on the bread slices and place them on the oven rack. Heat the bread for five minutes.

6. Arrange the heated bread slices on a plate. Top the slices with vegetables.

7. Serve immediately.

Spinach Parmesan Balls

Total Prep & Cooking Time: Thirty minutes

Yields: Ten servings

Nutrition Facts: Calories: 254.1 | Protein: 11.4g | Carbs: 18.4g | Fat: 14.2g | Fiber: 3.5g

Ingredients:

- Twenty ounces of frozen spinach (chopped)
- Two cups of bread crumbs
- One cup of parmesan cheese (grated)
- Half cup of butter (melted)
- Four green onions (chopped)
- Four eggs (beaten)
- Pepper and salt (for seasoning)

Method:

1. Start by preheating your oven at 175 degrees Celsius.

2. Take a bowl and combine spinach, bread crumbs, cheese, green onions, butter, pepper, salt, and eggs. Make balls of one-inch size from the prepared mixture.

3. Arrange the spinach balls on a baking tray. Bake for fifteen minutes until browned.

4. Serve hot.

Cheese Garlic Bread

Total Prep & Cooking Time: Thirty minutes

Yields: Eight servings

Nutrition Facts: Calories: 260 | Protein: 7.1g | Carbs: 29.7g | Fat: 11.4g | Fiber: 1.5g

Ingredients:

- Half cup of butter (melted)
- One tsp. of garlic salt
- One-fourth tsp. of rosemary (dried)
- One-eighth tsp. of each
    - Basil (dried)
    - Thyme (dried)
    - Garlic powder
- One tbsp. of parmesan cheese (grated)
- One loaf of French bread (halved)

Method:

1. Preheat oven at 150 degrees Celsius.

2. Mix garlic salt, butter, basil, rosemary, thyme, garlic powder, and cheese in a bowl.

3. Spread the butter mixture on the halves of the bread. Add extra cheese from the top if you want to.

4. Place halves of bread on a baking tray. Bake for twelve minutes until browned.

Stuffed Mushrooms

Total Prep & Cooking Time: Forty-five minutes

Yields: Twelve servings

Nutrition Facts: Calories: 89 | Protein: 2.6g | Carbs: 1.3g | Fat: 8.9g | Fiber: 0.6g

Ingredients:

- Twelve whole mushrooms
- One tbsp. of each
  - Minced garlic
  - Vegetable oil
- Eight ounces of cream cheese (softened)
- One-fourth cup of parmesan cheese (grated)
- One-fourth tsp. of each
  - Onion powder
  - Black pepper (ground)
  - Cayenne powder (ground)

Method:

1. Preheat the oven to 175 degrees Celsius. Grease a baking tray with the help of cooking spray.

2. Clean the mushrooms using a damp kitchen towel; break the stems. Chop the mushroom stems finely.

3 Take a skillet and heat oil in it. Add chopped stems of mushroom and garlic—Cook for five minutes.

4. Remove the skillet from heat and let it cool. Add the cream cheese, black pepper, parmesan cheese, cayenne powder, and onion powder. Mix well.

5. Use a small spoon for filling the mushroom caps with the mushroom stuffing.

6. Place the mushroom caps on the prepared baking tray.

7. Bake for twenty minutes until liquid forms under the mushroom caps.

Tomato Bruschetta

Total Prep & Cooking Time: Thirty-five minutes

Yields: Twelve servings

Nutrition Facts: Calories: 214.1 | Protein: 10.6g | Carbs: 23.1g | Fat: 8.8g | Fiber: 2.6g

Ingredients:

- Six tomatoes (chopped)
- Half cup of sun-dried tomatoes
- Three garlic cloves (minced)
- One-fourth cup of olive oil
- Two tbsps. of balsamic vinegar
- One-third cup of basil
- One-fourth tsp. of each
  - Black pepper (ground)
  - Salt
- One baguette
- Two cups of mozzarella cheese (shredded)

Method:

1. Preheat your oven on the setting of broiler.

2. Combine tomatoes, olive oil, vinegar, garlic, sun-dried tomatoes, basil, pepper, and salt in a bowl. Let the mixture sit for ten minutes.

3. Cut the baguette into slices of a three-fourth inch. Arrange the baguette slices on a baking tray. Broil for two minutes until browned.

4. Add the mixture of tomatoes on the slices of bread and top with mozzarella cheese.

5. Broil again for five minutes.

Spicy Pumpkin Seeds

Total Prep & Cooking Time: One hour and ten minutes

Yields: Eight servings

Nutrition Facts: Calories: 91 | Protein: 3.2g | Carbs: 8.8g | Fat: 4.9g | Fiber: 0.7g

Ingredients:

- Two tbsps. of margarine
- Half tsp. of salt
- One-eighth tsp. of garlic salt
- Two tsps. of Worcestershire sauce
- Two cups of pumpkin seeds (raw)

Method:

1. Preheat your oven at 135 degrees Celsius.

2. Combine the ingredients in a mixing bowl.

3. Bake for one hour. Stir in between.

Chapter 3: Soups & Side Dishes Recipes

Soup forms an integral part of a vegetarian diet along with the side dishes. Here are some easy vegetarian recipes for side dishes and soups that you can include in your diet.

Carrot Soup
Total Prep & Cooking Time: Forty-five minutes

Yields: Four servings

Nutrition Facts: Calories: 351 | Protein: 3.2g | Carbs: 23.1g | Fat: 29.7g | Fiber: 4.2g

Ingredients:

- Two tbsps. of olive oil
- Four-hundred grams of carrots (cut in disks of half-inch)
- Half onion (diced)

- Four cloves of garlic (smashed)
- Two tsps. of cumin seeds
- Four cups of vegetable stock
- Two bay leaves
- One tsp. of salt
- One-fourth tsp. of white pepper
- Two tsps. of honey
- One-fourth cup of yogurt

Method:

1. Take a heavy bottom pan and add oil in it. Add onions, garlic, and cumin to the pan. Sauté on a medium flame for six minutes until tender and golden in color. Stir occasionally.

2. Add the stock, carrots, salt, bay leaves, white pepper, and simmer the mixture. Cover the pan and simmer for twenty minutes. Allow the soup to cool down for five minutes.

3. Use an immersion blender for blending the soup. Blend until you reach a silky smooth consistency.

4. Return the soup to heat and add honey. Stir the soup. Add yogurt and simmer. Taste the soup and adjust the seasonings. Keep the soup warm on very low flame until you serve.

5. Divide the soup among serving bowls. Serve with a dollop of yogurt from the top.

Note: You can use ground spices in place of the whole spices. But, whole spices will help in adding extra flavor.

Celery Soup

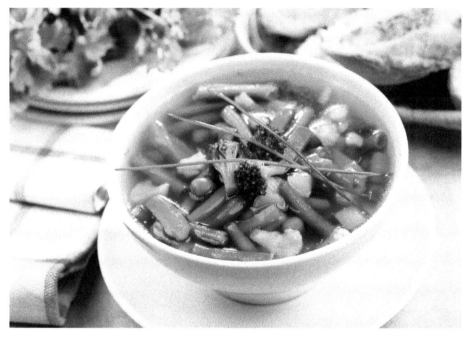

Total Prep & Cooking Time: Thirty-five minutes

Yields: Seven servings

Nutrition Facts: Calories: 180 | Protein: 4.2g | Carbs: 23.1g | Fat: 9.2g | Fiber: 4.9g

Ingredients:

- Two tbsps. of olive oil
- One onion (diced)
- Four cloves of garlic (chopped)
- Six cups of celery (thinly sliced)
- Two cups of potatoes (sliced in rounds)

- Four cups of vegetable stock
- One cup of water
- One bay leaf
- One tsp. of salt
- Half tsp. of pepper
- One-third tsp. of cayenne
- Half cup of sour cream
- One-fourth cup of each
  - Parsley (small stems)
  - Dill (small stems)

Method:

1. Take a large pot and add oil in it. Heat the oil and start adding the onion. Cook for five minutes until golden.

2. Roughly chop celery, potatoes, and garlic. Add garlic and cook the mixture for two minutes. Add potatoes, celery, stock, bay leaf, water, salt, cayenne, and pepper. The liquid needs to be enough to cover the vegetables. Cover the pot and boil the mixture. Simmer for ten minutes.

3. Remove bay leaf after turning off the stove. Add herbs to the pot and allow them to wilt.

4. Take an immersion blender and start blending the soup until silky smooth.

5. Return the pot to heat and cook over low flame for five minutes.

6. Serve with sour cream from the top.

Tomato Soup And Halloumi Croutons

Total Prep & Cooking Time: One hour and five minutes

Yields: Six servings

Nutrition Facts: Calories: 285 | Protein: 10.3g | Carbs: 13.2g | Fat: 23.2g | Fiber: 4.9g

Ingredients:

- Three pounds of tomatoes
- Half red onion (sliced in thin rings)
- Six cloves of garlic
- Two tsps. of thyme leaves

- One-third cup of oil
- Four cups of vegetable stock
- One-fourth cup of basil leaves (chopped)
- One cup of Greek yogurt

For croutons:

- One block of halloumi cheese (cut in cubes of three-fourth inch)
- One tbsp. of oil

Method:

1. Start by preheating your oven at 200 degrees Celsius.

2. Use parchment paper for lining baking sheet. Spread the onions, tomatoes, and garlic on the sheet. Drizzle with some oil from the top—roast in the oven for thirty minutes.

3. Heat some oil in a pan and start adding the halloumi cubes. Cook for four minutes until golden on all sides.

4. Add the roasted veggies in a pot along with the vegetable stock. Use an immersion blender for blending the soup until smooth. Place the pot over a low flame and add seasonings of your choice. Simmer the soup and add basil. Simmer for ten minutes.

5. Add half a cup of yogurt to the soup.

6. Serve the soup in serving bowls with croutons from the top.

Baked Potatoes And Mushrooms With Spinach

Total Prep & Cooking Time: Forty-five minutes

Yields: Four servings

Nutrition Facts: Calories: 235.1 | Protein: 7.1g | Carbs: 27.1g | Fat: 11.3g | Fiber: 4.9g

Ingredients:

- One pound of potatoes (halved)
- Three tbsps. of olive oil
- Half pound of Portobello mushroom
- Six garlic cloves
- Two tbsps. of thyme (chopped)
- One pinch of black pepper and salt
- One-fourth cup of cherry tomatoes
- Half cup of spinach (sliced)
- Two tbsps. of pine nuts (toasted)

Method:

1. Preheat your oven at 200/220 degrees Celsius.

2. Add the potatoes in a roasting pan and drizzle some oil from the top. Roast the potatoes for fifteen minutes.

3. Add mushrooms along with garlic to the pan. Add thyme from the top along with some olive oil. Sprinkle black pepper and salt. Roast again for five minutes.

4. Add cherry tomatoes to the pan. Cook again for five minutes until the mushrooms are tender.

5. Add toasted pine nuts from the top and serve with spinach by the side.

Garlic Potatoes

Total Prep & Cooking Time: Fifty minutes

Yields: Four servings

Nutrition Facts: Calories: 270.2 | Protein: 5.2g | Carbs: 39.7g | Fat: 12.1g | Fiber: 4.9g

Ingredients:

- Two pounds of red potatoes (quartered)
- One-fourth cup of butter (melted)
- Two tsps. of garlic (minced)
- One tsp. of salt
- One lemon (juiced)
- One tbsp. of parmesan cheese (grated)

Method:

1. Start by preheating the oven at 175 degrees Celsius.

2. Place the potatoes in a baking dish.

3. Combine butter, lemon juice, garlic, and salt in a small bowl. Add this mixture over the potatoes and stir for coating. Add parmesan cheese from the top.

4. Bake the potatoes by covering the dish in the preheated oven for thirty minutes. Remove the cover and bake again for ten minutes.

Buttery Carrots

Total Prep & Cooking Time: Twenty-five minutes

Yields: Four servings

Nutrition Facts: Calories: 182.3 | Protein: 0.8g | Carbs: 21.3g | Fat: 10.3g | Fiber: 3.9g

Ingredients:

- One pound of baby carrots
- One-fourth cup of margarine
- One-third cup of brown sugar

Method:

1. Cook the baby carrots in boiling water. Drain most of the liquid leaving behind a little bit of liquid at the base.

2. Remove the carrots from the pot. Add brown sugar along with margarine. Simmer the mixture for two minutes and add the carrots to the pot. Toss well for combining.

3. Serve warm.

Chapter 4: Main Course Recipes

After you are done with the soups and side dishes, now it is time to jump into the main course. Here are some tasty main course recipes that you can include within your vegetarian diet plan.

Nut And Tofu Loaf

Total Prep & Cooking Time: One hour and forty minutes

Yields: Six servings

Nutrition Facts: Calories: 308.3 | Protein: 15.2g | Carbs: 27.6g | Fat: 14.2g | Fiber: 4.8g

Ingredients:

- One serving of cooking spray
- Twelve ounces of tofu (firm, drained, cubed)
- Two large eggs
- One ounce dry mix of onion soup
- One tbsp. of soy sauce
- Three-fourth cup of walnuts (chopped)
- One tsp. of olive oil
- Eight ounces of fresh mushrooms (sliced)
- One onion (chopped)
- Two celery stalks (chopped)
- Two tsps. of oregano (dried)
- One and a half tsps. of basil (dried)
- Half tsp. of sage (dried)
- Two cups of bread crumbs

Method:

1. Start by preheating the oven at 175 degrees Celsius. Use a cooking spray for greasing loaf pan.

2.	Place eggs, tofu, soy sauce, and onion soup mix in a blender. Blend the ingredients until properly combined. Add the walnuts and blend again. Transfer the mixture of tofu to a bowl.

3.	Take a large skillet and heat oil in it. Add mushrooms and cook them for four minutes. Add celery and cook for two minutes—season with basil, sage, and oregano.

4.	Stir bread crumbs and veggies into the mixture of tofu. Press the loaf mixture into the pan.

5.	Bake the loaf in the oven for sixty to seventy minutes.

6.	Let the loaf cool down for five minutes before serving.

7.	Slice the loaf and serve warm.

Velvety Chickpea Curry

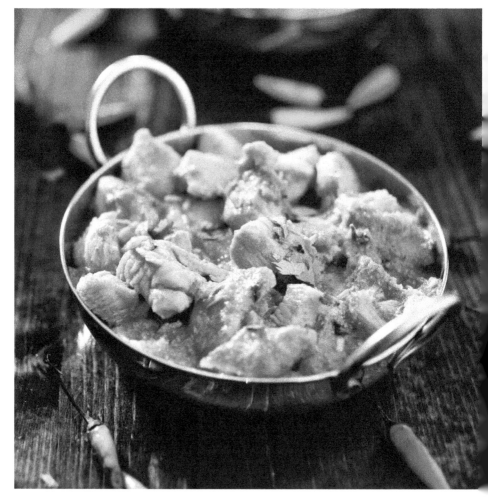

Total Prep & Cooking Time: Forty-five minutes

Yields: Six servings

Nutrition Facts: Calories: 408.3 | Protein: 10.2g | Carbs: 68.3g | Fat: 11.2g | Fiber: 8.9g

Ingredients:

- One tbsp. of each
  - Ginger root (minced)
  - Coconut oil
- One onion (sliced)
- Four garlic cloves (minced)
- Two tbsps. of curry powder
- One-fourth tsp. of pepper flakes
- Three cups of vegetable stock
- Two tbsps. of each
  - Soy sauce
  - Tomato paste
  - Maple syrup
- Half pound of potatoes (cut in pieces of a three-fourth inch)
- One carrot (sliced)
- Four cups of cauliflower florets
- One can of chickpeas (rinsed)
- Half cup of coconut milk
- One-fourth cup of cilantro (chopped)
- Half cup of peas (frozen)
- Salt (for seasoning)

Method:

1. Take a heavy-based pot and melt coconut oil in it. Add onions to the pot and sauté for five minutes. Add garlic and ginger to the pot—Cook for thirty seconds. Add pepper flakes, curry powder, soy sauce, stock, tomato paste, and maple syrup. Stir well.

2. Add carrots and potatoes to the pot and cover. Boil the mixture. Slightly open the cover and simmer for ten minutes. Add chickpeas, cauliflower, cilantro, and coconut milk. Stir well for combining. Simmer again for seven minutes. Add peas and cook for one minute.

3. Season with salt and cook for one minute.

4. Serve with basmati rice and cilantro from the top.

Tofu Pad Thai

Total Prep & Cooking Time: Forty-five minutes

Yields: Four servings

Nutrition Facts: Calories: 451 | Protein: 15.4g | Carbs: 60.1g | Fat: 15.2g | Fiber: 4.2g

;

Ingredients

- Twelve ounces of tofu (drained, cubed)
- One tbsp. of cornstarch
- Three tbsps. of vegetable oil
- Eight ounces of rice noodles

For the sauce:

- One-fourth cup of each
  - Sriracha sauce
  - Water
  - Soy sauce
- Two tbsps. of white sugar
- One tbsp. of tamarind concentrate
- One tsp. of pepper flakes
- One large egg
- Two tbsps. of spring onions (chopped)
- One and a half tbsp. of peanuts (crushed)
- One lime (cut in wedges)

Method:

1. Coat the tofu cubes with cornstarch in a large bowl.

2. Heat two tbsps. of oil in a skillet. Fry the coated tofu for two minutes on each side.

3. Place the rice noodles in a medium bowl. Cover the noodles using hot boiling water. Soak the noodles until soft for three minutes. Drain the water.

4. Mix sriracha sauce, water, sugar, soy sauce, pepper flakes, and tamarind concentrate in a skillet. Cook for five minutes.

5. Heat one tbsp. of oil in a large wok. Add noodles, onion, along with the tofu. Cook the mixture for three minutes. Add sauce and toss it for combining.

6. Push the noodles to a side and crack the egg in the center. Stir for thirty seconds and mix with the noodles.

7. Serve with peanuts, green onion, and wedges of lime.

Eggplant Parmesan

Total Prep & Cooking Time: One hour

Yields: Ten servings

Nutrition Facts: Calories: 480.2 | Protein: 21.2g | Carbs: 60.1g | Fat: 15.2g | Fiber: 9.8g

Ingredients:

- Three eggplants (sliced)
- Two eggs (beaten)
- Four cups of bread crumbs
- Six cups of spaghetti sauce
- Sixteen ounces of mozzarella cheese (shredded)
- Half cup of parmesan cheese
- Half tsp. of basil (dried)

Method:

1. Preheat the oven at 175 degrees Celsius.

2. Dip the slices of eggplant in egg and then coat in bread crumbs.

3. Arrange the slices of eggplant in a baking sheet and bake for five minutes on both sides.

4. Take a baking dish and spread the spaghetti sauce for covering the base. Arrange the eggplant slices over the sauce. Sprinkle cheese from the top. Repeat for the remaining layers. Top with basil and cheese.

5. Bake for thirty-minutes until browned.

Veg Korma

Total Prep & Cooking Time: Fifty-five minutes

Yields: Four servings

Nutrition Facts: Calories: 451 | Protein: 8.4g | Carbs: 40.1g | Fat: 30.2g | Fiber: 8.7g

Ingredients:

- Two tbsps. of vegetable oil
- One onion (diced)
- One tsp. of ginger root (minced)
- Four garlic cloves (minced)
- Two potatoes (cubed)
- Four carrots (cubed)
- One jalapeno pepper (sliced)
- Three tbsps. of cashews (ground)
- One can of tomato sauce
- Two tsps. of salt
- One and a half tbsps. of curry powder
- One cup of green peas (frozen)
- One red bell pepper (roughly chopped)
- One-third yellow bell pepper (roughly chopped)
- One bunch of cilantro
- Half cup of heavy cream

Method:

1. Take a skillet and heat oil in it. Add onions to the oil and cook until soft. Add garlic and ginger to the skillet. Cook for one minute. Add carrots, potatoes, cashews, jalapenos, and tomato sauce. Add curry powder and season with salt. Stir well and cook for ten minutes until the potatoes are soft.

2. Add bell pepper, peas, and cream. Lower the flame and cover the skillet—Cook for ten minutes.

3. Serve with cilantro from the top.

Mac And Cheese
Total Prep & Cooking Time: Fifty minutes

Yields: Six servings

Nutrition Facts: Calories: 456 | Protein: 24g | Carbs: 33.1g | Fat: 24.9g | Fiber: 2.3g

Ingredients:

- Two cups of elbow macaroni (uncooked)
- One-fourth cup of butter
- Two tbsps. of flour
- One tsp. of each
  o Black pepper (ground)
  o Mustard powder
- Two cups of milk
- Eight ounces of each
  o Cheese food (cubed)
  o American cheese (cubed)
- Half cup of bread crumbs

Method:

1. Preheat the oven at 180/200 degrees Celsius. Take a casserole dish and grease with butter.

2. Boil water in a pot with salt. Add the pasta and cook the pasta for six minutes. Drain the water.

3. Take a saucepan. Melt butter in it. Add mustard powder, flour, and pepper. Add milk and stir constantly. Add the cheeses and mix for two minutes until the sauce thickens.

4. Add the macaroni to the cheese mixture. Mix well.

5. Transfer the pasta mixture to the greased dish. Add bread crumbs from the top.

6. Bake for twenty minutes by covering the dish.

7. Serve hot.

Sesame Noodles

Total Prep & Cooking Time: Thirty minutes   Yields: Eight servings

Nutrition Facts: Calories: 365.2 | Protein: 7.3g | Carbs: 51.1g | Fat: 13.2g | Fiber: 3.9g

Ingredients:

- Sixteen ounces of linguine pasta
- Six garlic cloves (minced)
- Six tbsps. of each
  - Safflower oil
  - Sugar
  - Rice vinegar
  - Soy sauce
- Two tsps. of chili sauce
- Two tbsps. of sesame oil
- Six green onions (sliced)
- One tsp. of sesame seeds (toasted)

Method:

1. Boil water in a large pot along with some salt. Add the pasta. Keep cooking for eight minutes. Drain all the water.

2. Take a saucepan and heat oil in it. Add garlic, sugar, soy sauce, chili sauce, and sesame oil. Boil the mixture until the sugar gets dissolved.

3. Add the sauce to the cooked pasta and toss well for combining.

4. Serve with sesame seeds and green onions from the top.

Chapter 5: Dessert Recipes

Having a great dessert after a tasty meal can make you, as well as your stomach, feel good. So, here are some vegetarian dessert recipes for you.

Raspberry And Rosewater Sponge Cake

Total Prep & Cooking Time: Fifty-five minutes

Yields: Ten servings

Nutrition Facts: Calories: 441 | Protein: 4.1g | Carbs: 51.3g | Fat: 23.1g | Fiber: 1.3g

Ingredients:

- Two-hundred grams of butter (softened)
- Two-hundred and fifty grams of caster sugar
- Four eggs (beaten)
- One tsp. of vanilla extract
- Two cups of flour

For the rose filling:

- Half cup of double cream
- One tsp. of rosewater
- Four tbsps. of raspberry jam
- One-third cup of raspberries (crushed)

For rose icing:

- Half cup of icing sugar
- Half tsp. of rosewater

Method:

1. Heat the oven at 160 degrees Celsius.

2. Use parchment paper for lining two baking tins—grease with butter.

3. Mix sugar and butter in a bowl. Add the eggs and mix again.

4. Add vanilla extract to the egg mixture and mix. Add flour and fold.

5. Divide the cake batter into the prepared baking tins and bake in the oven for twenty minutes. Let the cakes cool for ten minutes.

6. Whisk double cream along with rosewater. Add the jam and mix.

7. Place one of the cakes on a serving plate and add the cream mixture. Add raspberries from the top and place the other cake on top.

8. Mix all the ingredients for the icing.

9. Serve the cake with rose icing from the top.

Easy Tiramisu

Total Prep & Cooking Time: One hour and fifteen minutes

Yields: Two servings

Nutrition Facts: Calories: 741 | Protein: 11.3g | Carbs: 44.3g | Fat: 51.6g | Fiber: 1.9g

Ingredients:

- Three tsps. of coffee granules
- Three tbsps. of coffee liqueur
- One and a half cup of mascarpone
- Half cup of condensed milk
- Six sponge fingers
- One tbsp. of cocoa powder

Method:

1. Mix coffee granules in two tbsps. of boiling water and stir for combining. Add three tbsps. of cold water along with coffee liqueur. Pour the mixture in a dish and keep aside.

2. Beat condensed milk, mascarpone, and vanilla extract in a bowl using a hand blender.

3. Break the fingers into two pieces and soak them in the mixture of coffee for thirty seconds.

4. Take a sundae glass and add the sponge fingers at the base. Add the cream mixture on top. Sift cocoa powder and chill in the refrigerator for one hour.

Chocolate Marquise

Total Prep & Cooking Time: Two hours and fifty-five minutes

Yields: Ten servings

Nutrition Facts: Calories: 710.3 | Protein: 7.8g | Carbs: 59.8g | Fat: 53g | Fiber: 1.5g

Ingredients:

- Three-hundred grams of dark chocolate
- Half cup of each
  - Caster sugar
  - Butter (softened)
- Six tbsps. of cocoa powder
- Six eggs
- One-third cup of double cream
- One-fourth cup of mint chocolate

Method:

1. Break the dark chocolate in small pieces and melt it using a double boiler system.

2. Beat butter and sugar in a bowl until creamy.

3.   Separate the egg whites and yolks.

4.   Mix the yolks with the sugar mixture until creamy.

5.   Whip the double cream in another bowl.

6.   Add the melted chocolate in the mixture of butter and fold gently. Add the whipped cream and mix well.

7.   Spoon the mixture of chocolate in a piping bag.

8.   Take a baking tin and pipe one layer of chocolate at the base of the tin. Cover the tin with pieces of mint chocolate. Repeat for the other layers. You will need to make four layers of mint chocolate.

9.   Cover the tin with a cling film.

10. Chill the marquise in the fridge for two hours.

11. Remove the marquise from the tin by using a sharp knife.

12. Serve by cutting into slices.

Lemon Syllabub

Total Prep & Cooking Time: Fifteen minutes

Yields: Four servings

Nutrition Facts: Calories: 328 | Protein: 2.2g | Carbs: 14.6g | Fat: 28.6g | Fiber: 0.2g

Ingredients:

- Two cups of whipping cream
- Half cup of caster sugar
- Three tbsps. of white wine
- Half a lemon (juice and zest)
- Berries (for serving)

Method:

1. Mix sugar and whipping cream in a bowl. Whip until soft peaks are formed.

2. Add white wine in the mixture. Mix well. Add lemon juice and lemon zest in the mixture. Combine the ingredients properly.

3. Spoon the mixture into serving bowls or glasses.

4. Sprinkle remaining lemon zest from the top.

5. Serve the lemon syllabub with berries.

Note: You can use a mix of berries or only one type of berry.

PART IV

Chapter 1: Meal Planning 101

Sticking to a diet is something that is not the easiest in the world. When it comes down to it, we struggle to change up our diets on a whim. It might be that for the first few days, you are able to stick to it and make sure that you are only eating those foods that are better for you, but over time, you will get to a point where you feel the pressure to cave in. You might realize that sticking to your diet is difficult and think that stopping for a burger on your way home won't be too bad. You might think that figuring out lunch or dinner is too much of a hassle, or you realize that the foods that you have bought forgot a key ingredient that you needed for dinner.

The good news is, you have an easy fix. When you are able to figure out what you are making for yourself for your meals well in advance, you stop having to worry so much about the foods that you eat, what you do with them, and what you are going to reach for when it's time to eat. You will be able to change up what you are doing so that you can be certain that the meals that you are enjoying are good for you, and you won't have to worry so much about the stress that goes into it. Let's take a look at what you need to do to get started with meal planning so that you can begin to do so without having to think too much about it.

Make a Menu

First, before you do anything, make sure that you make a menu! This should be something that you do on your own, or you should sit down with your family to ask them what they prefer. If you can do this, you will be able to ensure that you've got a clear-cut plan. When you have a menu a week in advance, you save yourself time and money because you know that all of your meals will use ingredients that are similar, and you won't have to spend forever thinking about what you should make at any point in time.

Plan around Ads

When you do your menu, make it a point to glance through the weekly ads as well. Typically, you will find that there are plenty of deals that you can make use of that will save you money.

Go Meatless Once Per Week

A great thing to do that is highly recommended on the Mediterranean Diet is to have a day each week where you go meatless for dinner. By doing so, you will realize that you can actually cut costs and enjoy the foods more at the same time. It is a great way to get that additional fruit and veggie content into your day, and there are plenty of healthy options that are out there for you. You just have to commit to doing so. In the meal plans that you'll see below, you will notice that there will be a meatless day on Day 2 every week.

Use Ingredients That You Already Have On Hand

Make it a point to use ingredients that you already have on hand whenever possible. Alternatively, make sure that all of the meals that you eat during the week use very similar ingredients. When you do this, you know that you're avoiding causing any waste or losing ingredients along the way, meaning that you can save money. The good news is, on the Mediterranean diet, there are plenty of delicious meals that enjoy very similar ingredients that you can eat.

Avoid Recipes that Call for a Special Ingredient

If you're trying to avoid waste, it is a good idea for you to avoid any ingredients in meals that are not going to carry over to other meals during your weekly plan. By avoiding doing so, you can usually save yourself that money for that one ingredient that would be wasted. Alternatively, if you find that you really want that dish, try seeing if you can freeze some of it for later. When you do that, you can usually ensure that your special ingredient at least didn't go to waste.

Use Seasonal Foods

Fruits and veggies are usually cheaper when you buy them in season, and even better, when you do so, you will be enjoying a basic factor of the Mediterranean diet just by virtue of enjoying the foods when they are fresh. Fresher foods are usually tastier, and they also tend to carry more vitamins and minerals because they have not had the chance to degrade over time.

Make Use of Leftovers and Extra Portions

One of the greatest things that you can do when it comes to meal planning is to make use of your leftovers and make-ahead meals. When you do this regularly, making larger portions than you need, you can then use the extras as lunches and dinners all week long, meaning that you won't have to be constantly worrying about the food that you eat for lunch. We will use some of these in the meal plans that you will see as well.

Eat What You Enjoy

Finally, the last thing to remember with your meal plan is that you ought to be enjoying the foods that are on it at all times. When you ensure that the foods that you have on your plate are those that you actually enjoy, sticking to your meal plan doesn't become such a chore, and that means that you will be able to do better as well with your own diet. Your meal plan should be loaded up with foods that you are actually excited about enjoying. Meal planning and dieting should not be a drag—you should love every moment of it!

Chapter 2: 1 Month Meal Plan

This meal plan is designed to be used for one month to help you simplify making sure that you have delicious meals to eat without having to think. These meals are fantastic options if you don't know where to start but want to enjoy your Mediterranean diet without much hassle. For each of the five weeks included, you will get one breakfast recipe, one lunch recipe, one dinner recipe, and one snack recipe to make meal planning a breeze. So, give these recipes a try! Many of them are so delicious, you'll want to enjoy them over and over again!

Week 1: Success is no accident—you have to reach for it

Mediterranean Breakfast Sandwich

Serves: 4

Time: 20 minutes

Ingredients:

- Baby spinach (2 c.)

- Eggs (4)

- Fresh rosemary (1 Tbsp.)

- Low-fat feta cheese (4 Tbsp.)

- Multigrain sandwich thins (4)

- Olive oil (4 tsp.)

- Salt and pepper according to preference

- Tomato (1, cut into 8 slices)

Instructions:

1. Preheat your oven. This recipe works best at 375° F. Cut the sandwich things in half and brush the insides with half of your olive oil. Place the things on a baking sheet and toast for about five minutes or until the edges are lightly browned and crispy.

2. In a large skillet, heat the rest of your olive oil and the rosemary. Use medium-high heat. Crack your eggs into the skillet one at a time. Cook until the whites have set while keeping the yolks runny. Break the yolks and flip the eggs until done.

3. Serve by placing spinach in between two sandwich thins, along with two tomato slices, an egg, and a tablespoon of feta cheese.

Greek Chicken Bowls

Serves: 4

Time: 20 minutes

Ingredients:

- Arugula (4 c.)
- Chicken breast tenders (1 lb.)

- Cucumber (1, diced)
- Curry powder (1 Tbsp.)
- Dried basil (1 tsp.)
- Garlic powder (1 tsp.)
- Kalamata olives (2 Tbsp.)
- Olive oil (1 Tbsp.)
- Pistachios (0.25 c., chopped)
- Red onion (half, sliced)
- Sunflower seeds (0.25 c.)
- Tzatziki sauce (1 c.)

Instructions:

1. In a bowl, mix in the chicken tenders, curry powder, dried basil, and garlic powder. Make sure to coat the chicken evenly.
2. Heat one tablespoon of olive oil over medium-high. Add the chicken and cook for about four minutes on each side. Remove from the pan and set aside to cool.
3. Place one cup of arugula into four bowls. Toss in the diced cucumber, onion, and kalamata olives.
4. Chop the chicken and distribute evenly between the four bowls.
5. Top with tzatziki sauce, pistachio seeds, and sunflower seeds.

Ratatouille

Serves: 8

Time: 1 hour 30 minutes

Ingredients:

- Crushed tomatoes (1 28 oz. can)
- Eggplants (2)
- Fresh basil (4 Tbsp., chopped)
- Fresh parsley (2 Tbsp., chopped)
- Fresh thyme (2 tsp.)
- Garlic cloves (4, minced and 1 tsp, minced)
- Olive oil (6 Tbsp.)
- Onion (1, diced)
- Red bell pepper (1, diced)
- Roma tomatoes (6)
- Salt and pepper to personal preference
- Yellow bell pepper (1, diced)
- Yellow squashes (2)
- Zucchinis (2)

Instructions:

1. Get your oven ready. This recipe works best at 375° F.
2. Slice the tomatoes, eggplant, squash, and zucchini into thin rounds and set them to the side.

3. Heat up two tablespoons of olive oil in an oven safe pan using medium-high heat. Sauté your onions, four cloves of garlic, and bell peppers for about ten minutes or when soft. Add in your pepper and salt along with the full can of crushed tomatoes. Add in two tablespoons of basil. Stir thoroughly.

4. Take the vegetable slices from earlier and arrange them on top of the sauce in a pattern of your choosing. For example, a slice of eggplant, followed by a slice of tomato, squash, and zucchini, then repeating. Start from the outside and work inward to the center of your pan. Sprinkle salt and pepper overtop the veggies.

5. In a bowl, toss in the remaining basil and garlic, thyme, parsley, salt, pepper, and the rest of the olive oil. Mix it all together, and spoon over the veggies.

6. Cover your pan and bake for 40 minutes. Uncover and then continue baking for another 20 minutes.

Snack Platter

Serves: 6

Time:

Ingredients:

Rosemary Almonds

- Butter (1 Tbsp.)

- Dried rosemary (2 tsp.)
- Salt (pinch)
- Whole almonds (2 c.)

Hummus

- Chickpeas (1 15 oz. can, drained and rinsed)
- Garlic clove (1, peeled)
- Lemon (half, juiced)
- Olive oil (2 Tbsp.)
- Salt and pepper according to personal preference
- Tahini (2 Tbsp.)
- Water (2 Tbsp.)

Other sides

- Bell pepper (1, sliced)
- Cucumber (1, sliced)
- Feta cheese (4 oz, cubed)
- Kalamata olives (handful, drained)
- Pepperoncini peppers (6, drained)
- Pitas (6, sliced into wedges)
- Small fresh mozzarella balls (18)
- Soppressata (6 oz.)
- Sweet cherry peppers (18)

Instructions:

1. To get started, make your rosemary almonds. Take a large skillet and place it on a burner set to medium heat. Start melting the butter in, then toss in the almonds, rosemary and a bit of salt. Toss the nuts on occasion to ensure even coating.

2. Cook the almonds for roughly ten minutes, getting them nicely toasted. Set the almonds off to the side to let them cool.

3. Now you'll set out to make the hummus. Take a blender or food processor and toss in the hummus ingredients. Blend until you get a nice, smooth paste. If you find that your paste is too thick, try blending in a bit of water until you get the desired consistency. Once you have the right consistency, taste for seasoning and adjust as necessary.

4. Pour and scrape the hummus into a bowl and drizzle in a bit of olive oil. Set it off to the side to get the rest of the platter going.

5. Grab the sweet cherry peppers and stuff them with the little balls of mozzarella. Arrange a platter in any pattern you like. If serving for a party or family, try keeping each snack in its own little segment to keep things looking neat.

Week 2: Self-belief and effort will take you to what you want to achieve

Breakfast Quesadilla

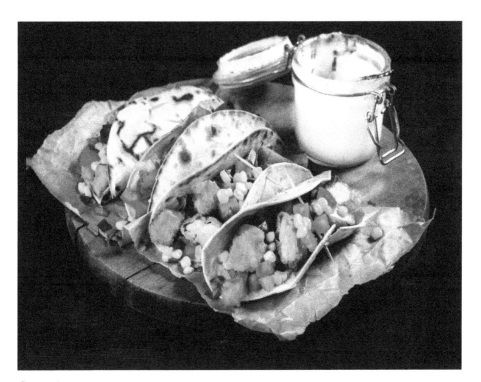

Serves: 1

Time: 10 minutes

Ingredients:

- Basil (handful)
- Eggs (2)
- Flour tortilla (1)

- Green pesto (1 tsp.)
- Mozzarella (0.25 c.)
- Salt and pepper according to personal preference
- Tomato (half, sliced)

Instructions:

1. Scramble your eggs until just a little runny. Remember, you will be cooking them further inside the quesadilla. Season with salt and pepper.
2. Take the eggs and spread over half of the tortilla.
3. Add basil, pesto, mozzarella cheese, and the slices of tomato.
4. Fold your tortilla and toast on an oiled pan. Toast until both sides are golden brown.

Greek Orzo Salad

Serves: 6

Time: 25 minutes

Ingredients:

- Canned chickpeas (1 c., drained and rinsed)
- Dijon mustard (0.5 tsp)
- Dill (0.33 c., chopped)
- Dried oregano (1 tsp)
- English cucumber (half, diced)
- Feta cheese crumbles (0.5 c.)
- Kalamata olives (0.33 c., halved)
- Lemon (half, juice and zest)
- Mint (0.33 c., chopped)
- Olive oil (3 Tbsp.)
- Orzo pasta (1.25 c. when dry)
- Roasted red pepper (half, diced)
- Salt and pepper to taste
- Shallot (0.25 c., minced)
- White wine vinegar (2 Tbsp.)

Instructions:

1. Prepare the orzo according to the packaging details. Once the orzo is al dente, drain it and rinse until it drops to room temperature.
2. In a bowl, toss all the ingredients together until thoroughly incorporated.

One Pot Mediterranean Chicken

Serves: 4

Time: 1 hour

Ingredients:

- Chicken broth (3 c.)
- Chicken thighs (3, bone in, skin on)

- Chickpeas (1 15 oz can, drained and rinsed)
- Dried oregano (0.5 tsp.)
- Fresh parsley (2 Tbsp., chopped)
- Garlic cloves (2, minced)
- Kalamata olives (0.75 c., halved)
- Olive oil (2 tsp.)
- Onion (1, finely diced)
- Orzo pasta (8 ounces uncooked)
- Roasted peppers (0.5 c., chopped)
- Salt and pepper according to personal preference

Instructions:

1. Prepare your oven at 375°. Heat your olive oil in a large skillet over medium-high heat.
2. Season the chicken with salt and pepper on both sides. Toss the chicken into the skillet and cook for five minutes on each side, or until golden in color. Remove the chicken.
3. Take the skillet and drain most of the rendered fat, leaving about a teaspoon. Add the onion and cook for five minutes. Toss in the garlic and cook for an additional minute.
4. Now you will want to add the orzo, roasted peppers, oregano, chickpeas, and olives into the pan. Add in salt and pepper.
5. Place the thighs on top of the orzo and pour in the chicken broth.
6. Bring to a boil, then cover and place in the oven. Bake for 35 minutes or until chicken has cooked through. Top with parsley and serve.

Mediterranean Nachos

Serves: 6

Time: 10 minutes

Ingredients:

- Canned artichoke hearts (1 c., rinsed, drained, and dried)
- Canned garbanzo beans (0.75 c., rinsed, drained, and dried)
- Feta cheese (0.5 c., crumbled)
- Fresh cilantro (2 Tbsp., chopped)
- Pine nuts (2.5 Tbsp.)
- Roasted red peppers (0.5 c., dried)
- Sabra Hummus (half of their 10 oz. container)
- Tomatoes (0.5 c., chopped)
- Tortilla chips (roughly half a bag)

Instructions:

1. Get your oven ready by setting it to 375°F. In a baking pan, layer the tortilla chips, and spread hummus over them evenly. Top with garbanzo beans, red peppers, artichoke hearts, feta cheese, and pine nuts.
2. Bake for about five minutes or until warmed through. Remove the baking pan and top the nachos with fresh cilantro and tomatoes. Serve and enjoy.

Week 3: The harder you work, the greater the success

Breakfast Tostadas

Serves: 4

Time: 15 minutes

Ingredients:

- Beaten eggs (8)
- Cucumber (0.5 c., seeded and chopped)
- Feta (0.25 c., crumbled)
- Garlic powder (0.5 tsp)
- Green onions (0.5 c., chopped)
- Oregano (0.5 tsp)
- Red Pepper (0.5 c., diced)
- Roasted red pepper hummus (0.5 c.)
- Skim milk (0.5 c.)
- Tomatoes (0.5 c., diced)
- Tostadas (4)

Instructions:

1. In a large skillet, cook the red pepper for two minutes on medium heat until softened. Toss in the eggs, garlic powder, milk, oregano, and green onions. Stir constantly until the egg whites have set.
2. Top the tostadas with hummus, egg mixture, cucumber, feta, and tomatoes.

Roasted Vegetable Bowl

Serves: 2

Time: 45 minutes

Ingredients:

- Crushed red pepper flakes (a pinch)
- Fresh parsley (1 Tbsp., chopped)
- Kalamata olives (0.25 c.)
- Kale (1 c., ribboned)
- Lemon juice (1 Tbsp.)
- Marinated artichoke hearts (0.25 c., drained and chopped)
- Nutritional yeast (1 Tbsp.)
- Olive oil (1 Tbsp., then enough to drizzle)
- Salt and pepper to taste

- Spaghetti squash (half, seeds removed)
- Sun-dried tomatoes (2 Tbsp., chopped)
- Walnuts (0.25 c., chopped)

Instructions:

1. Get your oven ready by setting it to 400° F. Take a baking sheet and blanket it with parchment paper.
2. Take the squash half and place it on the parchment paper. Drizzle olive oil over the side that is cut, and season with salt and pepper. Turn it over so it is facing cut side down and bake for 40 minutes. It is ready when it is soft.
3. Remove the squash shell, and season with a bit more salt and pepper.
4. Stack the kale, artichoke hearts, walnuts, sun-dried tomatoes, and kalamata olives on the squash.
5. Squeeze the lemon juice over and drizzle olive oil. Finish with chopped parsley and a bit of crushed red pepper flakes.

Mediterranean Chicken

Serves: 4

Time: 40 minutes

Ingredients:

- Chicken breasts (1 lb., boneless, skinless)
- Chives (2 Tbsp., chopped)
- Feta cheese (0.25 c., crumbled)
- Garlic (1 tsp., minced)
- Italian seasoning (1 tsp.)
- Lemon juice (2 Tbsp.)
- Olive oil (2 Tbsp., and 1 Tbsp.)
- Salt and pepper according to personal preference
- Tomatoes (1 c., diced)

Instructions:

1. Pour in two tablespoons of olive oil, the lemon juice, salt, pepper, garlic, and Italian seasoning in a resealable plastic bag. Add in the chicken, seal and shake to coat the chicken.
2. Allow the chicken to marinate for at least 30 minutes in the refrigerator.
3. Heat the rest of the olive oil in a pan over medium heat.
4. Place the chicken on the pan and cook for five minutes on each side, or until cooked through.
5. In a bowl, mix the tomatoes, chives, and feta cheese. Season with salt and pepper.
6. When serving, spoon the tomato mixture on top of the chicken.

Baked Phyllo Chips

Serves: 2

Time: 10 minutes

Ingredients:

- Grated cheese (your choice)
- Olive oil (enough to brush with)
- Phyllo sheets (4)
- Salt and pepper according to personal preference

Instructions:

1. Get your oven ready by setting it to 350° F. Brush olive oil over a phyllo sheet generously. Sprinkle grated cheese and your seasoning on top.
2. Grab a second sheet of your phyllo and place it on top of the first one. Again, brush with olive oil and sprinkle cheese and seasoning on top.
3. Repeat this process with the remaining sheets of phyllo. Top the stack with cheese and seasoning.
4. Once complete, cut the stack of phyllo into bite-sized rectangles. A pizza cutter may be helpful here.
5. Grab a baking sheet and blanket it with some parchment paper. Take your phyllo rectangles and place them on the parchment paper.
6. Bake in the oven for about seven minutes or until they reach a golden color.
7. Remove them from the oven and allow them to cool before serving.

Week 4: You don't need perfection—you need effort

Mini Omelets

Serves: 8

Time: 40 minutes

Ingredients:

- Cheddar cheese (0.25 c., shredded)
- Eggs (8)
- Half and half (0.5 c.)
- Olive oil (2 tsps.)
- Salt and pepper according to personal preference
- Spinach (1 c., chopped)

Instructions:

1. Get your oven ready by setting it to 350° F. Prepare a muffin pan or ramekins by greasing them with olive oil.
2. In a bowl, beat the eggs and dairy until you have a fluffy consistency.
3. Stir in the cheese and your seasonings. Pour in the spinach and continue beating the eggs.
4. Pour the egg mixture into your ramekins or muffin pan.
5. Bake the omelets until they have set, which should be roughly 25 minutes. Remove them from the oven and allow them to cool before serving.

Basil Shrimp Salad

Serves: 2

Time: 40 minutes

Ingredients:

- Dried basil (1 tsp.)
- Lemon juice (1 Tbsp.)
- Olive oil (1 tsp.)
- Romaine lettuce (2 c.)
- Shrimp (12 medium or 8 large)
- White wine vinegar (0.25 c.)

Instructions:

1. Whisk together the white wine vinegar, olive oil, lemon juice, and basil. Stick your shrimp in the marinade for half an hour.
2. Take the marinade and shrimp and cook in a skillet over medium heat until cooked through.
3. Allow the shrimp to cool along with the juice and pour into a bowl. Toss in the romaine lettuce and mix well to get the flavor thoroughly infused in the salad. Serve.

Mediterranean Flounder

Serves: 4

Time: 40 minutes

Ingredients:

- Capers (0.25 c.)
- Diced tomatoes (1 can)
- Flounder fillets (1 lb.)
- Fresh basil (12 leaves, chopped)
- Fresh parmesan cheese (3 Tbsp., grated)
- Garlic cloves (2, chopped)
- Italian seasoning (a pinch)
- Kalamata olives (0.5 c., pitted and chopped)
- Lemon juice (1 tsp.)

- Red onion (half, chopped)
- White wine (0.25 c.)

Instructions:

1. Set your oven to 425° F. Take a skillet and pour in enough olive oil to sauté the onion until soft. Cook on medium-high heat.
2. Toss in the garlic, Italian seasoning, and tomatoes. Cook for an additional five minutes.
3. Pour in the wine, capers, olives, lemon juice, and only half of the basil you chopped.
4. Reduce the heat to low and stir in the parmesan cheese. Simmer for ten minutes or until the sauce has thickened.
5. Place the flounder fillets in a baking pan and pour the sauce over top. Sprinkle the remaining basil on top and bake for 12 minutes.

Nutty Energy Bites

Serves: 10

Time: 10 minutes

Ingredients:

- Dried dates (1 c., pitted)
- Almonds (0.5 c.)

- Pine nuts (0.25 c.)
- Flaxseeds (1 Tbsp., milled) Porridge oats (2 Tbsp.)
- Pistachios (0.25 c., coarsely ground)

Instructions:

1. Take the dates, pine nuts, milled flaxseeds, almonds, and porridge oats and pour them into a food processor or blender. Mix until thoroughly incorporated.
2. Using a tablespoon, scoop the mixture and roll it between your hands until you have a small, bite-sized ball. Do this until you have used the entirety of the dough. This recipe should be enough for about ten.
3. On a plate, sprinkle your ground pistachios. Take the energy balls and roll them on the pistachio grounds, making sure to coat them evenly. Serve or store in the refrigerator.

Week 5: Transformation Happens One Day at a Time

Mediterranean Breakfast Bowl

Serves: 1

Time: 25 minutes

Ingredients:

- Artichoke hearts (0.25 c., chopped)
- Baby arugula (2 c.)
- Capers (1 Tbsp)
- Egg (1)
- Feta (2 Tbsp., crumbled)
- Garlic (0.25 tsp)
- Kalamata olives (5, chopped)
- Lemon thyme (1 Tbsp., chopped)
- Olive oil (0.5 Tbsp.)
- Pepper (0.25 tsp)
- Sun-dried tomatoes (2 Tbsp., chopped)
- Sweet potato (1 c., cubed)

Instructions:

1. Take your olive oil and, when hot, pan fry your sweet potatoes for 5-10 minutes until they have softened. Then, sprinkle on the seasonings.
2. Place arugula into a bowl, then top with potatoes, then everything but the egg.
3. Prepare the egg to your liking and serve.

Chicken Shawarma Pita Pockets

Serves: 6

Time: 40 minutes

Ingredients:

- Cayenne (0.5 tsp)
- Chicken thighs (8, boneless, skinless, bite-sized pieces)
- Cloves (0.5 tsp, ground)
- Garlic powder (0.75 Tbsp.)
- Ground cumin (0.75 Tbsp.)
- Lemon juice (1 lemon)
- Olive oil (0.33 c.)
- Onion (1, sliced thinly)
- Paprika (0.75 Tbsp.)
- Salt
- Turmeric powder (0.75 Tbsp.)

To serve:

- Pita pockets (6)
- Tzatziki sauce
- Arugula
- Diced tomatoes
- Diced onions
- Sliced Kalamata olives

Instructions:

1. Combine all spices. Then, place all chicken, already diced, into the bowl. Coat well, then toss in onions, lemon juice, and oil. Mix well and let marinade for at least 3 hours, or overnight.

2. Preheat the oven to 425 F. Allow chicken to sit at room temperature a few minutes. Then, spread it on an oiled sheet pan. Roast for 30 minutes.

3. To serve, fill up a pita pocket with tzatziki, chicken, arugula, and any toppings you prefer. Enjoy.

Turkey Mediterranean Casserole

Serves: 6

Time: 35 minutes

Ingredients:

- Fusilli pasta (0.5 lbs.)
- Turkey (1.5 c., chopped)
- Sun dried tomatoes (2 Tbsp., drained)
- Canned artichokes (7 oz., drained)
- Kalamata olives (3.5 oz., drained and chopped)
- Parsley (0.5 Tbsp., chopped and fresh)
- Basil (1 T, fresh)
- Salt and pepper to taste
- Marinara sauce (1 c.)

- Black chopped olives (2 oz., drained)
- Mozzarella cheese (1.5 c., shredded)

Instructions:

1. Warm your oven to 350 F. Prepare your pasta according to the directions, drain, and place into a bowl. Prepare your basil, parsley, olives, tomatoes, artichokes, and other ingredients.

2. Mix together the pasta with the turkey, tomatoes, olives, artichokes, herbs, seasoning, and marinara sauce. Give it a good mix to incorporate all of the ingredients evenly.

3. Take a 9x13 oven-safe dish and layer in the first half of your pasta mixture. Then, sprinkle on half of your mozzarella cheese. Top with the rest of the pasta, then sprinkle on the chopped black olives as well. Spread the rest of the shredded cheese on top, then bake it for 20-25 minutes. It is done when the cheese is all bubbly and the casserole is hot.

Heirloom Tomato and Cucumber Toast

Serves: 2

Time: 5 minutes

Ingredients:

- Heirloom tomato (1, diced)
- Persian cucumber (1, diced)
- Extra virgin olive oil (1 tsp)
- Oregano (a pinch, dried)
- Kosher salt and pepper
- Whipped cream cheese (2 tsp)
- Whole grain bread (2 pieces)
- Balsamic glaze (1 tsp)

Instructions:

4. Combine the tomato, cucumber, oil, and all seasonings together.
5. Spread cheese across bread, then top with mixture, followed by balsamic glaze.

Chapter 3: Maintaining Your Diet

Sticking to a diet can be tough. You could see that other people are having some great food and wish that you could enjoy it too. You might realize that you miss the foods that you used to eat and feel like it's a drag to not be able to enjoy them. When you are able to enjoy the foods that you are eating, sticking to your diet is far easier. However, that doesn't mean that you won't miss those old foods sometimes. Thankfully, the Mediterranean diet is not a very restrictive one—you are able to enjoy foods in moderation that would otherwise not be allowed, and because of that, you can take the slice of cake at the work party, or you can choose to pick up a coffee for yourself every now and then. When you do this, you're not doing anything wrong, so long as you enjoy food in moderation.

Within this chapter, we are going to take a look at several tips that you can use that will help you with maintaining your diet so that you will be able to stick to it, even when you feel like things are getting difficult. Think of this as your guide to avoiding giving in entirely—this will help you to do the best thing for yourself so that you can know that you are healthy. Now, let's get started.

Find Your Motivation

First, if you want to keep yourself on your diet, one of the best things that you can do is make sure that you find and stick to your motivation. Make sure that you know what it is in life that is motivating you. Are you losing weight because a doctor told you to? Fair enough—but how do you make that personal and about yourself? Maybe instead of looking at it as a purely health-related choice, look at it as something that you are doing because of yourself. Maybe you are eating better so that you are able to watch your children graduate or so that you can run after them at the park and stay healthy, even when it is hard to do so.

Remind Yourself Why You are Eating Healthily

When you find that you are struggling to eat healthily, remind yourself of why you are doing it in the first place. When you do this enough, you will begin to resist the urges easier than ever. Make it a point to tell yourself not to eat something a certain way. Take the time to remind yourself that you don't need to order that greasy pizza—you are eating better foods because you want to be there for your children or grandchildren.

Reminding yourself of your motivation is a great way to overcome those cravings that you may have at any point in time. The cravings that you have are usually strong and compelling, but if you learn to overcome them, you realize that they weren't actually as powerful as you thought they were. Defeat the cravings. Learn to tell yourself that they are not actually able to control you. Tell yourself that you can do better with yourself.

Eat Slowly

Now, on the Mediterranean diet, you should already be eating your meals with other people anyway. You should be taking the time to enjoy those meals while talking to other people and ensuring that you get that connection with them, and in doing so, you realize that you are able to do better. You realize that you are able to keep yourself under control longer, and that is a great way to defend and protect yourself from overeating.

When you eat slowly, you can get the same effect. Eating slowly means that you will have longer for your brain to realize that you should be eating less. When you are able to trigger that sensation of satiety because you were eating slowly, you end up eating fewer calories by default, and that matters immensely.

Keep Yourself Accountable

Don't forget that, ultimately, your diet is something that you must control on your own. Keep yourself accountable by making sure that you show other people what you are doing. If you are trying to lose weight, let them know, and tell them how you plan to do so. When you do this, you are able to remind yourself that other people know what you are doing and why—this is a great way to foster that sense of accountability because you will feel like you have to actually follow through, or you will be embarrassed by having to admit fault. You could also make accountability to yourself as well. When you do this, you are able to remind yourself that your diet is your own. Using apps to track your food and caloric intake is just one way that you can do this.

Remember Your Moderation

While it can be difficult to face a diet where you feel like you can't actually enjoy the foods that you would like to eat, the truth is that on the Mediterranean diet, you are totally okay to eat those foods that you like or miss if you do so in moderation. There is nothing that is absolutely forbidden on the Mediterranean diet—there are just foods that you should be restricting regularly. However, that doesn't mean that you can't have a treat every now and then.

Remembering to live in moderation will help you from feeling like you have to cheat or give up as well. When you are able to enjoy your diet and still enjoy the times where you want to enjoy your treats, you realize that there is actually a happy medium between sticking to the diet and deciding to quit entirely.

Identify the Difference between Hunger and Craving

Another great way to help yourself stick to your diet is to recognize that there is a very real difference between actually being hungry and just craving something to eat. In general, cravings are felt in the mouth—when you feel like you are salivating or like you need to eat something, but it is entirely in your head and mouth, you know that you have a craving. When you are truly hungry, you feel an emptiness in your stomach—you are able to know because your abdomen is where the motivation is coming from.

Being able to tell when you have a craving and when you are genuinely hungry, you can usually avoid eating extra calories that you didn't actually need. This is major—if you don't want to overeat, you need to know when your body actually needs something and when it just wants something. And if you find that you just want something, that's okay too—just find a way to move on from it. If you want to indulge a bit here and there, there's no harm in that!

Stick to the Meal Plan

When it comes to sticking to a diet, one of the easiest and most straightforward ways to do so is to just stick to your meal plan that you set up. You have it there for a reason—it is there for you to fall back on, and the sooner that you are willing to accept that, recognizing that ultimately, you can stay on track when you don't have to think about things too much, the better you will do. You will be able to succeed on your diet because you will know that you have those tools in place to protect you—they will be lined up to ensure that your diet is able to provide you with everything that you need and they will also be there so that you can know that you are on the right track.

Drink Plenty of Water

Another key to keeping yourself on track with your diet is to make sure that you drink plenty of water throughout the day. Oftentimes, we mistake our thirst with hunger and eat instead. Of course, if you're thirsty, food isn't going to really fix your problem, and you will end up continuing to mix up the sensation as you try to move past it. The more you eat, the thirstier you will get until you realize that you're full but still feeling "hungry." By drinking plenty of water any time that you think that you might want to eat, you will be able to keep yourself hydrated, and in addition, you will prevent yourself from unintentionally eating too much.

Eat Several Times Per Day

One of the best ways to keep yourself on track with your diet is to make sure that you are regularly eating. By eating throughout the day, making sure that you keep yourself full, it is easier to keep yourself strong enough to resist giving in to cravings or anything else. When you do this regularly, you will discover that you can actually keep away much of your cravings so that you are more successful in managing your diet.

Eating several times per day often involves small meals and snacks if you prefer to do so. Some people don't like doing this, but if you find that you're one of those people who will do well on a diet when you are never actually hungry enough to get desperate enough to break it, you will probably be just fine.

Fill Up on Protein

Another great way to protect yourself from giving in and caving on your diet is to make sure that you fill up on protein. Whether it comes from an animal or plant source, make sure that every time you eat, you have some sort of tangible protein source. This is the best way to keep yourself on track because protein keeps you fuller for longer. When you eat something that's loaded up with protein, you don't feel the need to eat as much later on. The protein is usually very dense, and that means that you get to resist feeling hungry for longer than you thought that you would.

Some easy proteins come from nuts—but make sure that you are mindful that you do not end up overeating during this process—you might unintentionally end up eating too many without realizing it. While you should be eating proteins regularly, make sure that you are mindful of calorie content as well!

Keep Only Healthy Foods

A common mistake that people make while dieting is that they end up caving when they realize that their home is filled up with foods that they shouldn't be eating. Perhaps you are the only person in your home that is attempting to diet. In this case, you may end up running into a situation where you have all sorts of non-compliant foods on hand. You might have chips for your kids or snacks that your partner likes to eat on hand. You may feel like it is difficult for you to stay firm when you have that to consider, and that means that you end up stuck in temptation.

One of the best ways to prevent this is to either cut all of the unhealthy junk out of your home entirely or make sure that you keep the off-limits foods in specific places so that you don't have to look at it and see it tempting you every time that you go to get a snack for yourself. By trying to keep yourself limited to just healthy foods, you will be healthier, and you will make better decisions.

Eat Breakfast Daily

Finally, make sure that breakfast is non-negotiable. Make sure that you enjoy it every single day, even if you're busy. This is where those make-ahead meals can come in handy; by knowing that you have to keep to a meal plan and knowing that you already have the food on hand, you can keep yourself fed. Breakfast sets you up for success or failure—if you want to truly succeed on your diet, you must make sure that you are willing to eat those healthier foods as much as possible, and you must get started on the right foot. Enjoy those foods first thing every day. Eat so that you are not ravenous when you finally do decide that it is time to sit down and find something to eat. Even if you just have a smoothie or something quick to eat as you go, having breakfast will help you to persevere.

CPSIA information can be obtained
at www.ICGtesting.com
Printed in the USA
LVHW010430271020
669864LV00017B/285

9 789814 950701